THE MILFORD SERIES
POPULAR WRITERS OF TODAY
ISSN 0163-2469
VOLUME SIXTY-EIGHT

Running from the Hunter

The Life and Works of
CHARLES BEAUMONT

by

Lee Prosser

Edited by Miguel Alcalde

R. REGINALD
The Borgo Press
San Bernardino, California □ MCMXCVI

THE BORGO PRESS
Publishers of Fine Books Since 1975
Post Office Box 2845
San Bernardino, CA 92406
United States of America

*   *   *   *   *   *   *   *

Library of Congress Cataloging-in-Publication Data

Prosser, Harold Lee, 1944-
  Running from the hunter : the life and works of Charles Beaumont / by
Lee Prosser.
    p. cm. — (The Milford series. Popular writers of today, ISSN 0163-
2469 ; v. 68)
  Includes bibliographical references and index.
  ISBN 0-89370-191-2 (cloth). — ISBN 0-89370-291-9 (pbk.)
  1. Beaumont, Charles, 1929-1967. 2. Authors, American—20th century—
Biography. 3. Fantastic literature, American—History and criticism. I.
Title. II. Series.
PS3552.E2316Z82 1996
813'.54—dc20   95-5346
                                                                                CIP

FIRST EDITION

CONTENTS

DEDICATION

This book is dedicated to:
William F. Nolan, Charles Beaumont, Robert Bloch,
William Shatner, Gerina Dunwich, Swami Chetanananda,
J. N. Williamson, Ray Bradbury, Jack Finney, Poul
Anderson, Simon Perchik, Don Bachardy, Jerry L.
Anderson, Stephen King, James Gunn, Louis Owens, Jack
Williamson, Mary A. Burgess, Chad Oliver, Ray Russell,
Robert Reginald, Richard Matheson, Christopher
Isherwood, Whitley Strieber, Scott Cunningham, Michael
Harner, Christopher Cabot, Yvonne Frost, and Barbara A.
Quarton

A CHARLES BEAUMONT CHRONOLOGY

1929 Charles Leroy Nutt born January 2, 1929 at Chicago, Illinois, son of Charles Hiram Nutt and Violet "Letty" Phillips. His father worked for the railroad, and his mother had once been a "scenarist" at Essanay Studios in Hollywood.

1930 (through 1940) Beaumont grows up on Chicago's north side; he attends grade school in Chicago, playing football and studying piano.

1941 Charles discovers "the world of books" when he is stricken with a two-year bout of spinal meningitis. Late in 1941, he and his mother go to live with his grandmother and aunts at Everett, Washington.

1942 Beaumont spends much of the year bedridden, reading voraciously, and writing "critical" letters to the science fiction pulp magazines. He becomes a dedicated SF fan.

1943 More of his letters are printed in the pulps, where he is now signing himself Charles "McNutt." He has a collaborative cartoon published in *Fantastic Adventures* (October issue).

1944 Charles attends Everett High School, specializing in drama. He also acts on a local radio station, and declares his goal of becoming a professional writer in a school booklet, "My Vocation."

1945 The author uses the name "E. T. Beaumont" for the cover art on a fanzine published by Forrest J Ackerman. He forms a local science fiction fan club, and writes, edits, and publishes his own amateur fan magazine, *Utopia*. He has a radio show on station KRKO in Everett, for which he writes, directs, and acts. He takes a bus trip to Los Angeles to interview his idol, Fritz Lang (director of *Metropolis*), and plans to write a full biography of this master director.

1946 At the age of 17, Charles leaves high school a year short of graduation, to enlist in the U.S. Army Infantry; after serving three months, he is given a medical discharge for a bad back. Later this year, in Los Angeles again, he works as an inker for the animation department of MGM Studios. He writes and directs his own fifteen-minute radio show of movieland chatter, *Hollywood Hi-Lights*. He is also a featured actor on *Drama Workshop*. Beaumont meets writer Ray Bradbury at an L.A. bookstore; Bradbury becomes a mentor and literary role model.

1947 As "Charles McNutt," the author is profiled in the "Tops Among Teens" feature in the *Chicago Tribune*. He decides to pursue an acting career, and attends the Bliss-Hayden Drama School in Los Angeles on the G.I. bill. He stars in a local stage production of *Broadway* as "Charles Beaumont," the name he would eventually legally adopt as his own. With help from Fritz Lang, Charles is signed by Universal Studios as a contract actor—but no roles materialize. He also attends classes at the Art Center, and begins illustrating books and magazines for Bill Crawford's Fantasy Publishing Company, Inc. (FPCI).

1948 Beaumont abandons his acting career. His father (now living in Mobile, Alabama) helps him obtain a job as a railroad clerk in Mobile, where he meets his future wife, Helen Louise Broun (then age twenty).

6

1949 After a whirlwind courtship, he marries Helen in November, and they leave immediately for Los Angeles, where he unsuccessfully attempts to find work as a commercial artist. To make ends meet, he works as sign painter's assistant, a dishwasher, a theater usher, and as a tracing clerk for California Motor Express.

1950 Beaumont's first child, Christopher, is born in December. The author abandons art as a career, and moves to an apartment in North Hollywood, California. He returns to his first love, writing, and sells a short story to *Amazing Stories*, the Chicago-based pulp magazine whose editorial offices he used to "haunt" as a youngster. Charles performs (as a reader) on the student radio station at the University of Southern California.

1951 Beaumont's first professional story, "The Devil, You Say," is published in *Amazing Stories* (January). Beaumont takes a job as a multilith operator in the Music Department at Universal Studios. He meets writer Richard Matheson.

1952 A second story, "The Beautiful People," is published in *Worlds of If*. He buys an MG-TC automobile, establishing his early interest in sports cars and racing. Beaumont meets aspiring author William F. Nolan.

1953 Beaumont is fired from his office job (June), and decides to become a full-time writer. Two stories appear this year. He wins the Jules Verne Award for "The Beautiful People." Attends meetings of the Los Angeles Science Fantasy Society (LASFS). Forrest J Ackerman becomes his first literary agent.

1954 A breakthrough year: Beaumont makes his first sale to the slicks—to *Playboy*—in April, the same month that his first teleplay ("Masquerade," for the series

Four Star Playhouse) is aired. Eight short stories are published in 1954, including "Black Country" (*Playboy,* September); Beaumont makes his first sale to the Disney comic books. He works briefly as an Assistant Editor for Dell Comics.

1955 "Red Beans and Ricely Yours," Beaumont's first non-fiction sale to the high-paying *Playboy,* appears in that magazine's February issue, followed quickly by his classic, much-reprinted short stories, "The Hunger" (in the April issue) and "The Crooked Man" (in August). Beaumont quickly becomes a *Playboy* regular. Ten stories, including some of the author's best-known works of short fiction, are published this year. He becomes a columnist ("The Science Screen") for *The Magazine of Fantasy & Science Fiction* (continuing through December, 1957). He also begins attending local sports car racing events with William F. Nolan. He leaves the Ackerman Agency for a new agent, Don Congdon of New York City (whose agency continues to represent the Beaumont Estate to this day).

1956 Beaumont's second child (and first daughter), Catherine, is born in August. Beaumont makes his first sale to *Rogue,* another men's magazine, with a profile of actor Robert Mitchum (February). He acts as editor of the "Rogue of Distinction" profile series through 1959. Nine short stories appear in 1956. Beaumont sells his first sports racing article, reflecting his growing interest in that field. He is put on a $6,000-per-year "retainer" from *Playboy.*

1957 Beaumont begins his first novel, *Where No Man Walks* (never finished). Beaumont's first book, *The Hunger and Other Stories,* is published in cloth by G. P. Putnam's Sons (April), followed later the same year by Beaumont's first novel, the pseudonymous *Run from the Hunter* (co-authored with John Tomerlin). Letty Nutt, Beaumont's mother, dies in

8

July. He races his Porsche on the San Diego Circuit, and travels to Nassau, in the Bahamas, for the magazine *Speed Week*. Eighteen new stories appear this year, including eight original pieces in his collection, *The Hunger*.

1958 *Queen of Outer Space*, Beaumont's first produced screenplay, is released, starring Zsa Zsa Gabor. He takes a trip with his family to Europe (May). Two new books appear: *Yonder: Stories of Fantasy and Science Fiction*, and the anthology *Omnibus of Speed* (co-edited with William F. Nolan). Seven new stories apppear in 1958. Beaumont begins writing television scripts with Richard Matheson.

1959 "Perchance to Dream" (aired November 27) marks Beaumont's maiden sale to the new *Twilight Zone* TV series, beginning a long and successful relationship with Rod Serling. A major mainstream novel, *The Intruder*, is published by Putnam; six new stories are published this year. In March, he works in Michigan for director Otto Preminger on an unproduced screenplay.

1960 Beaumont's third child (second daughter), Elizabeth, is born in January. The last major new Beaumont story collection, *Night Ride and Other Journeys*, is published by Bantam, with four original short stories; this essentially marks the end of Beaumont's career as a fiction writer, seventy stories and two novels having been published during the preceding nine-year period. Henceforth he devotes most of his creative energies to television and screenwriting. Beaumont makes four more sales to *Twilight Zone*, and works at MGM for producer George Pal. He wins the *Playboy* Award for Best Article of 1960 published in that magazine, for "Chaplin." He travels to Europe (May) to cover the Monaco Grand Prix for *Playboy*.

9

1961 Roger Corman options Beaumont's novel, *The Intruder*, and begins filming it that summer in southern Missouri, with Beaumont adapting the screenplay, and acting in a minor role. Five more teleplays appear on Rod Serling's *Twilight Zone*. In April, his final short story for *Playboy*, "Blood Brother," appears. He races his new Porsche "Spyder" at Palm Springs.

1962 Publishes *The Fiend in You*, an anthology of fantasy and horror, for Ballantine Books. Three Beaumont screenplays are produced this year: *The Wonderful World of the Brothers Grimm, Burn, Witch, Burn!*, and *The Premature Burial*; three more Beaumont teleplays are produced for *The Twilight Zone*. *The Intruder* is released by Pathe-American. Beaumont teaches writing classes at UCLA. He writes a screen treatment for *The Mask of Fu Manchu* for MGM (unproduced).

1963 Beaumont's fourth child (and second son), Gregory, is born in June. Screen and television assignments are now coming faster than Beaumont can handle them, and he begins farming them out to various colleagues, and editing the results. By spring he seems continually harried, and by summer he seems unable to concentrate on his work. Friends notice that his short-term memory is slipping. Beaumont's last new short story, "Mourning Song," is published in the magazine *Gamma*, and later chosen for inclusion in *The 9th Annual of the Year's Best SF*. *The Haunted Palace*, a loose adaptation of Lovecraft's *The Strange Case of Charles Dexter Ward*, is produced by American-International. Seven teleplays, some ghostwritten by others, appear under Beaumont's name on *The Twilight Zone*. A major collection of his nonfiction pieces, *Remember? Remember?*, is published by Putnam. By year's end, he can no longer write, due to his growing illness.

1964 Beaumont is diagnosed (July) as having developed an exceptionally early case of Alzheimer's Disease; his friends step in to help support his family by developing literary and screen projects. Two Beaumont screenplays are produced: the classic film, *The Seven Faces of Dr. Lao* (with Tony Randall), and *The Masque of the Red Death,* plus two teleplays on the soon-to-be-cancelled *Twilight Zone.* An anthology of racing essays, *When Engines Roar* (co-edited with William F. Nolan), is published by Bantam Books.

1965 Beaumont's health declines to the point where he must be sent to the Motion Picture Country Home and Hospital (March). A retrospective story collection, *The Magic Man—and Other Science Fantasy Stories*, is assembled by his friends for publication by Fawcett Books. One final screenplay, *Mister Moses*, is produced by United Artists. The author's last *Playboy* articles, both ghostwritten and adapted from Beaumont ideas or notes, are published in February and July.

1966 *The Edge*, a collection of previously-published Beaumont stories, is assembled for the British market, and published by Panther Books.

1967 Charles Beaumont dies on February 21 at Woodland Hills, California, aged thirty-eight years.

1971 Helen Louise Beaumont dies of cancer (May), leaving their four underaged children orphaned. Christopher Beaumont attempts to keep the family together until he can turn twenty-one.

1975 *All Together Now*, a fictionalized account of the Beaumont children's efforts to remain a family unit, airs in February as an ABC Movie of the Week, to excellent critical reviews.

1982 *Best of Beaumont*, a new retrospective collection of Beaumont stories, including one previously unprinted short story, is published by Bantam Books (December); writer Ray Bradbury and eldest son Christopher Beaumont contribute moving memoirs.

1984 First appearance of Beaumont's autobiographical essay, "My Grandmother's Japonicas," on his teenage years in Everett, Washington, which is published in the horror anthology, *Masques*.

1986 *The Work of Charles Beaumont: An Annotated Bibliography & Guide*, by Beaumont's friend, William F. Nolan, is published by Borgo Press.

1988 A definitive collection of the author's stories, *Charles Beaumont: Selected Stories*, edited with a biographical introduction by Roger Anker, is published by Dark Harvest (August); this 400-page volume includes twenty-nine Beaumont stories (including five never before published), plus a chapter from *The Intruder*, and seventeen memoirs by Beaumont's writer friends and other associates.

1989 In its last issue, *The Twilight Zone Magazine* features a Beaumont section, with a new Beaumont story (one of the five new pieces in *Selected Stories*), plus new biographical memoirs by Roger Anker, William F. Nolan, George Clayton Johnson, and Chad Oliver. *Charles Beaumont: Selected Stories* wins a Bram Stoker Award from the Horror Writers of America for Best Collection of the Year.

1990 A previously unproduced Beaumont screenplay, *Brain Dead*, is released by Concorde Pictures. *The Work of Charles Beaumont: An Annotated Bibliography & Guide, Second Edition, Revised and Expanded*, by William F. Nolan, is published by Borgo Press, including the second appearance of Beaumont's autobiographical essay, "My Grandmother's Japonicas."

I.

INTRODUCTION AND INTERVIEWS

When Charles Beaumont (1929-1967) died tragically young, imaginative fiction lost one of its most important creative voices. Charles Beaumont, whose real name was Charles Leroy Nutt, also wrote under the pen names of Keith Grantland, C. B. Lovehill, and S. M. Tenneshaw, among others. He had a wry sense of humor and delighted in penetrating the fabric of societal concerns. Concerned with a fear of disease and early death, he used these two themes extensively throughout his writings. On a subtler level, his writing constantly exposed the foibles of modern society. He had a remarkable talent for investing ordinary situations with well-crafted characters, bizarre twists, and ironic endings that never failed to enchant his many devoted readers and friends. A friend of such accomplished American authors as Robert Bloch, William F. Nolan, Ray Russell, Chad Oliver, Ray Bradbury, George Clayton Johnson, Richard Matheson, Jerry Sohl, Anthony Boucher, and Rod Serling, he also associated with many individuals in the movie industry, including actor William Shatner and director George Pal. Beaumont's memory remains strong and vivid among his living peers.

A fellow writer who was not only a friend of the author, but who also left a lasting impression on some of Beaumont's fiction, was the late Robert Bloch. As a major contemporary writer of horror and suspense fiction and screen and teleplays, Bloch greatly influenced Beaumont. Both Beaumont and Bloch shared similar perspectives on different topics, and both men were also able to use their fiction to criticize society in their separate writings and screen works.

If Beaumont's true *métier* was fantasy, his second was mystery and suspense fiction. Whether he was writing fiction or nonfiction, or whether his work was entirely original or infused with the input of his fellow writers, the brilliant framework was essentially Beaumont's and reflected his own unique thoughts and visions.

A brief sketch of Charles Beaumont's life is in itself fascinating and the stuff from which movies are made. He was born on January 2, 1929 in Chicago, Illinois to Charles Hiram and Violet (Phillips) Nutt. He grew up in Chicago and Everett, Washington. His early childhood was marred by an attack of spinal meningitis at age twelve. He was a self-educated man and spent a brief period in the United States Army, receiving a medical discharge for a bad back. Beaumont attended the Bliss-Hayden Acting School in California on the GI Bill. He starred in a California version of the Hecht-MacArthur play, *Broadway*, under his now-legal last name of Beaumont, adopted from the French words "beau" (beautiful) and "mont" (mountain) because he liked the sound and because Beaumont made a better writing name than Nutt or McNutt. Hoping for an acting career in Hollywood, the author instead began inking MGM animated cartoons, and later worked in the mimeo room at Universal Studios. He was briefly signed by Universal Studios as an actor, but due to an aborted movie production in which he was to co-star, he abandoned the profession. His first professional writing sale was to *Amazing Stories* in 1950. He married Helen Broun, a remarkable and charming woman whom he met during 1948 while briefly employed as a railroad clerk in Mobile, Alabama. Their first child, Christopher, was born in 1950, and they had three more children born over the next thirteen years—Catherine, Elizabeth, and Gregory. A loving father, he was devoted to his family, and they always came first during hard times, Charles doing whatever he had to do to provide for their security and comfort. Fired from his position as a multilith operator at Universal Studios in June of 1953 at the age of twenty-four, Charles Beaumont accepted the challenge to become a full-time writer.

In April of 1954, Beaumont made his first major sale to the slicks with *Playboy*, and became one of the magazine's chief feature writers. By 1958, he was selling teleplays and motion picture scripts consistently to the TV and film industry. Rod Serling's *The Twilight Zone* debuted on television in 1959, and Charles Beaumont became one of Serling's chief writers.

By 1961 Charles Beaumont was at the height of his career. He wrote the screenplay from his novel for the Roger Corman film production of *The Intruder*, and himself played the role of the high school principal in this tense drama concerning Southern school integration. This electrifying drama also starred Beaumont's friends William Shatner as Adam Cramer, William F. Nolan as Bart Carey, George Clayton Johnson as Abner West, OCee Ritch as Jack Allardyce, Charles Barnes as Joey Green, and Frank Maxwell as Tom McDaniel. In his role as the high school principal, Harley Paton, Charles Beaumont gave his only performance as an actor in a motion picture. The movie was critically acclaimed for its texture and realism, and for its ruthless examination of the themes of racial prejudice and segregation. At this point in his career, Charles Beaumont had fully arrived after ten years of struggle: his fiction and nonfiction were appearing regularly, six of his books had been published, and he was in constant demand as a writer of film and television scripts. He had established a reputation for excellence and craftsmanship in the entertainment industry.

By the summer of 1963, however, the curtain was starting to fall prematurely upon Charles Beaumont's brilliant career and life. Normally an energetic man with a charismatic personality and open sincerity about his nature, Beaumont began abruptly to change. His friends began to notice that he was slowing down significantly, that he looked years older than his chronological age, that he had lost the ability to concentrate. Beaumont's last written short story, "Mourning Song," appeared in *Gamma* later that year. At the age of thirty-four, Beaumont's magic with words was lost, his writing stopped. Like a candle burning too brightly at both ends, his career disintegrated and extinguished itself.

In July of 1964, following exhaustive tests at the University of California, Los Angeles, the doctors there determined that Charles Beaumont was suffering from very early Alzheimer's Disease. A horrifying disease in its effects on the human mind and body, it gives its victims premature senility and an early death; there was—and is—no cure. By March of 1965 he was no longer able to remain at home with the family he loved so much, and was taken to the Motion Picture Country Home and Hospital in Woodland Hills, California for constant medical care in the final stages of his illness.

As a victim of Alzheimer's Disease in its final stage, Charles Beaumont felt no discomfort or pain, and he no longer knew who he was or who came to visit him; he had entered a world of gentle forgetfulness and blurred memories and ultimate disintegration of his mind. He died quietly at the Motion Picture Country Home and Hospital on February 21, 1967 at the young age of thirty-eight.

Charles Beaumont has been sadly neglected by academia, but deserves far better. This study is being written in the hope that it will spark new interest in his life and writings, that it will lead to additional studies of one of America's most gifted writers of the 1950s. Beaumont shattered many editorial taboos with his insightful work and helped make possible the honest discussion of such vital social topics as homosexuality ("The Crooked Man," 1955), racism and prejudice ("Black Country," 1954), and nonconformity ("The Beautiful People," 1952). He left behind two good novels: *Run from the Hunter* (1957), a classic suspense novel focusing on violence in American society, and *The Intruder* (1959), a still important treatment on the twin themes of racial prejudice and discrimination in the United States. At least two dozen of his moving short fictions and nostalgic essays remain highly readable and relevant today. His *Twilight Zone* scripts were among the best filmed for that series, and such motion picture scripts as *The Seven Faces of Doctor Lao* remain vivid and entertaining. Beaumont created a remarkable canon of work that

16

work that will intrigue and keep scholars busy for decades to come. Had he lived, he would have become one of America's leading mainstream writers.

Alzheimer's Disease killed Beaumont and silenced the magic of his words, but the ideas he expressed through his writings are as fresh today as when he first wrote them. An idea man who was carefully attuned to his times, he was a highly creative individual who enjoyed life to the fullest and was a true friend to those with whom he associated. With uncanny insight, he wrote about and predicted the revival in nostalgia long before the movement actually got underway; his nonfiction book, *Remember? Remember?*, a collection of poignant articles previously published in the slicks and collected in book form in 1963, fully illustrates this. Pursuit of a dream, loneliness, and death were three of his major themes.

That Charles Beaumont was an open, questioning, sincere individual is a certainty. Beaumont saw major social changes coming in American society, and his prophetic visions and social conscience infused his writings. He foresaw that technological society would lead to a lack of communication and role conflict between people. He once stated: "In older, simpler days, we were less leery of our emotions—possibly because we hadn't been tipped that they were signs of fraility."

In analyzing Charles Beaumont's writing, I have examined it from three perspectives: sociological, philosophical, and literary. I believe that Beaumont was an existential Christian, as will become apparent from the discussion that follows.

Major sociological themes in Beaumont's writings reflect the acculturation process that Beaumont went through with every American in the United States: definition of the situation, looking-glass self, anomie, alienation, cultural relativity, self-fulfilling prophecy, role conflict, role priorities, societal masks, depersonalization, significant others, paradoxical perception, reference group, and compartmentalization, among others.

Major literary themes in Beaumont's writings concern labeling and individuality: these are the qualities and attributes which set one person apart from others, whether in a societal, psychological, philosophical, or ethnic sense, or taken together; they include the ability or freedom to have a personal identity.

Major philosophical themes include death, conformity, nonconformity, ethics, logic, morality, magic, religion, illusion, and mysticism, among others. Given Charles Beaumont's preoccupation and fascination with death and disease and the processes of each, he could have become an expert medical sociologist had he pursued this career. As it was, his interest in such matters was almost prophetic on a personal level.

To understand how Beaumont's writings reflect the workings of the inner man, and to comprehend the messages in his writings, is to enter a strange, enchanting world that is both terrifying and beautiful at the same instant, a veritable Twilight Zone of the writer. The keys to unlocking its door are located within the structure of the author's plots and dialogue: each key opens an individual door to a vision as only Beaumont could create it, and behind the mask of each vision is the truth that he wants the reader to confront. A surface reading of his fiction will give the reader mere entertainment; an in-depth reading of his fiction will electrify the reader's imagination and increase his or her comprehension.

To delineate Charles Beaumont as Man and Writer, I solicited the following interviews from his contemporaries and peers, to provide appreciations and tributes to one of America's most ingenious writers. Each piece reflects how each individual perceived Beaumont during the time that he knew him:

PROSSER: Charles Beaumont (1929-1967) has been long neglected by academia, yet continues to fascinate and attract new readers to his writings nearly three decades after his death from Alzheimer's disease. He is finally being recognized for the genius he was. Why do you feel that it has taken so long for Beaumont to receive this long-overdue recognition?

ROBERT BLOCH: Recognition, either during a writer's lifetime or posthumously, occurs only when he finds a champion. Poe, although ignored here, was "discovered" after death by Charles Baudelaire and others in France; Bradbury's career soared after its recognition by writer Christopher Isherwood; August Derleth crusaded for the fiction of H. P. Lovecraft by establishing Arkham to publish Lovecraft's works; Derleth himself found an advocate in Sinclair Lewis. But Charles Beaumont wasn't touted by an important critic or literary figure during his lifetime, and died too soon to benefit from the attention which—in the years that followed—was bestowed on fantasy writers by academics and critics who began pushing their favorites in the pages of the many magazines devoted to the field which started publication during the past two decades or so. Beaumont simply slipped through the cracks and disappeared; and his reprinted work was lost in the shuffle amongst hundreds of other paperback publications. Like the late Henry Kuttner, Beaumont and his work were acknowledged but not considered "Important" by any eminent advocates.

RAY BRADBURY: Probably Beaumont suffers from what most of us in the field have suffered, lack of recognition because we worked in a field that was not, in the '50s and '60s anyway, recognized by the literary critics as important. It was only after '69 when we landed on the moon that we all began to get some attention. By then Chuck had been dead some few years and wasn't around to defend or promote himself. It looks as if we will have to be the ones to defend and promote him.

RICHARD MATHESON: I would say that one important reason is that Chuck Beaumont was never a category writer. Although his work is naturally associated with *The Twilight Zone*, and his story collections were visually presented as being of a fantastic nature, his creative output was not confined in any way to fantasy or science-fiction—or even to fiction for that matter; he wrote many articles and published a book of them entitled *Remember? Remember?* The scope of his script, prose, and article work was extremely broad, extending through a large variety of subjects and ideas. Since fame to a writer often seems to depend on that writer specializing within a narrow range of subject matter, Chuck's widely diverse output has, I think, mitigated against recognition of his talent. In brief, he has too many separate audiences instead of one big one.

CHAD OLIVER: I think there is a very slim connection between real talent and academic recognition. Chuck, God bless him, was a highly successful commercial writer who made a lot of money from the slicks like *Playboy* and from TV and films. That tends to turn academic critics off. His best work was still ahead of him: Chuck spent a lot of his early writing time on some quite average science fiction before he finally found his own voice. Tragically, he only had about fifteen years as a producing writer, and this at a time when critical interest in "popular" writers virtually did not exist. If Chuck had lived, the recognition would have come sooner. He had the ability and the energy to become a major American writer.

RAY RUSSELL: Three reasons, I think: first, the sort of periodicals he usually appeared in (genre pulps and men's magazines of the *Playboy* kind) are traditionally ignored by literary (if not sociological) academia. Second, his career was cut short so early by long illness and death that he was never able to produce enough work of the first rank. Finally, too much of his time was wasted on television.

* * * * * * *

PROSSER: Charles Beaumont was a perceptive, inquisitive individual, and much of his writing reflects his concern and interest in social themes. What do you feel is important about Charles Beaumont's writing to the history of American literature?

ROBERT BLOCH: Beaumont, like Kuttner, helped bring a sophistication of style and content to the fantasy field. He was a keen observer and social commentator—perhaps a little ahead of his time and the tastes of the general reading public. When he tackled homosexuality, for example, it was still a hush-hush subject for "popular" fiction. Gide could get away with it in books designed to appeal to the intelligentsia, but Beaumont's story appeared in *Playboy*. Only in retrospect is it possible for the average reader to realize just how incisive Beaumont's insights were—and are. Similarly, his avid interest in past performances—in print, on the airwaves and on screen—predated the upsurge of the "nostalgia" craze. Now a whole generation of nostalgia-buffs, both readers and critics, has arisen; if Beaumont had lived, his reputation would have soared accordingly. At the time his preoccupation was ignored or dismissed as of little consequence. But his analyses were valid then, and equally valid today. And his fantasy mirrors the reality of his times.

RAY BRADBURY: He was an imaginative writer with a wide range. Certainly his prolific short story output with a variety of subjects puts him in the company of such writers as John Collier. Above all, he was simply a wonderfully good, a damn good writer. Grand fun. And critics, of course, are afraid to have fun at their reading. Or so it seems with many of them.

RICHARD MATHESON: I believe that Chuck Beaumont created a meticulously polished lens through which he offered his readers remarkable views of the many regions of the human psyche. On this lens he threw a fierce light of perception which never faltered in its honest intensity. What we see in our minds because of this are belief-challenging, consciousness-altering visions which are often microscopic in nature. The presentation

21

of these visions to the readers of the world is the bed-rock of the importance of Charles Beaumont's writing to American literature.

CHAD OLIVER: First and foremost, it was his intoxication with words. He had a style that made his prose dance. Chuck was not a deep thinker, but he was alive to everything that happened around him. He was a caring, compassionate man without an ounce of pomposity in him. It was not so much *what* he wrote but *how* he wrote. The man could make words sing. That is no small accomplishment.

RAY RUSSELL: I think social themes played a small part in his work, and interested him only when they appealed to his taste for the sensational and melodramatic, of which he was a master. His chief values as a writer, in my opinion, were a strong sense of story, a vivid visual imagination, great facility, an enormous vocabulary, and a flexible, eclectic style.

* * * * * * *

PROSSER: Charles Beaumont had a wry sense of humor and lived a fascinating life. Was this the real Beaumont or part of his literary persona, or were both interwined, given the complexity of the man's intellect?

ROBERT BLOCH: Chuck's life may appear to be fascinating, but much of it was grim indeed. Initially saddled with the surname of "Nutt," burdened by poor health as a child, disappointed in his hopes for an acting career, victimized by ripoffs in his early attempts at scriptwriting, bedevilled by the necessity of grinding out material to meet deadlines, and doomed to early death under harrowing circumstances, he had far from the easy life which outsiders believe to be the lot of the Hollywood writer. No wonder he developed a "wry" sense of humor; it was necessary armor. His interests surfaced in his stories and scripts, of course, and to a certain extent reflect his private *persona*, but in his work he usually maintained the posture of the performer without fully revealing the intent of inner anguish. Nonetheless, he left a legacy in print which partially portrays the attributes of a man whose friendship I still cherish.

RAY BRADBURY: The real Beaumont was the real Beaumont. What you see is what you get. I never detected any split between the fascinating, the curious, the wry Beaumont, and his stories. He loved to throw confetti in the air, run under it, and see what colors landed on his shoulders, his eyelids, and his nose!

RICHARD MATHESON: First came the "real" Beaumont—to whatever extent the "reality" of any human being can be ascertained. Then came the literary persona, a derivation of the real person. There can be no church-state separation between person and writer. Indeed, by a skillfully analyzed compilation of a writer's lifelong output, the human being beneath may well be discovered in far more minute detail than therapy could elicit; this I firmly believe. The complexity of Charles Beaumont's intellect lies hidden in the fabric of his written works.

CHAD OLIVER: Look, it takes a special kind of flair for a man to change his name from Nutt to Beaumont and set out to become a Writer in capital letters. Chuck had his problems in coping with his relatively sudden success, and he was a sick man for several years before he died. But of all the writers I have known, Chuck was the happiest and most secure at what he was doing. The real Beaumont was full of verve and fun and enthusiasm. Don't, I pray you, turn him into a demon-haunted caricature. I can still hear his laughter, and I assure you that it was genuine. All writers have a dark side, but there was more zest in Chuck than despair.

RAY RUSSELL: I'm not sure I understand the question, but I'll try to answer it in this way: it's true that he did have a wry sense of humor in his personal life, as well as in his work. As for a "fascinating life," he was not a two-fisted, icon-smashing wild man, but he liked to live well, dress well, have a good time with his friends, and in the privacy of his fantasies, undoubtedly he lived a "fascinating," adventurous life, which he drew upon for his stories. Like most writers, he was an outsider, an observer, rather than a participant. (As Joseph Conrad wrote in *Lord Jim*, "The onlookers see most of the game.") Some may say he was flamboyant, reckless, devil-may-care, but I never saw him that way. Yes, he occasionally raced cars—but it was a hobby much less hazardous than his more precarious profession, free-lance writing.

II.

AUTOBIOGRAPHICAL SKETCHES

Only one major autobiographical work by Charles Beaumont has been published. "My Grandmother's Japonicas," a detailed account of his boyhood first published in 1984, is important to any study of Beaumont, for it reveals Beaumont's early fascination with death and illness. In this short work, Beaumont discusses people who died in his grandmother's rooming house in Everett, Washington, and the effect of these deaths upon him. It is a sensitive, moving account, and no complete understanding of Beaumont as man or writer is possible without reading it.

Although "My Grandmother's Japonicas" is the only major autobiographical work written by Beaumont to see publication, other material exists that may come to light at a later date. Good autobiographical writing reveals a writer's background and influences, and in Beaumont's interesting case, it reveals the writer's essence. Beaumont was known to be a prolific letter writer, and a book collection of Beaumont's letters would probably be the literary shocker of the decade should it ever come to pass.

Certain autobiographical material about Beaumont must be mentioned in order for the reader to understand more fully this author's complex personality. Beaumont had three favorite contemporary authors: Irwin Shaw, Dylan Thomas, and John Steinbeck. Beaumont had planned to write a play with Richard Matheson on the life of Dylan Thomas. Beaumont was ever a stylist, and insisted that his written images reflect his most important feelings as to time, place, locale, and emotion. If there is one writer that influenced Beaumont's style in this regard, it was Dylan Thomas.

Beaumont was known for his brilliant mind and ability to absorb facts quickly. He had a remarkable memory for faces as well, and was familiar with every bit actor in Hollywood. He knew and associated with numerous celebrities and was friends with such rising stars as William Shatner and Scott Brady. Between an illusion and the truth was "Beaumont's Greater Truth," which improvised on what really happened and was an elaboration of a particular event. He possessed a keen instinct for literary trends, was an organizer, and he hated being alone.

Beaumont was also a natural mimic and enjoyed imitating accents and voices. Born with an incredibly complex ear for music, Beaumont could pick up any tune, and loved to whistle the themes of the symphonies he favored. He was addicted to jazz and classical music. He liked art but was better suited to writing and eventually abandoned a commercial art career.

Known as a sexual athlete and a ladies' man during his bachelor days, Beaumont loved beautiful women, but settled readily into the role of husband and father with devotion and loyalty. When he married Helen, he did not venture from his nuptial bed during their short, happy life together. Despite his good looks and charismatic manner, Beaumont's relationships with other women after his marriage remained platonic only. He considered his wife and family the most important things in his life, and he was a very affectionate and kind individual.

In a live television interview given to "Cavalcade of Books" in 1959 when Beaumont was thirty years old, he discussed his then-new novel, *The Intruder*. He revealed his lifelong interest in character analysis, knew intuitively that integration would come to pass, and stated that certain facets of his background and experience served as the building blocks for his portrayal of Adam Cramer and the New South.

Beaumont also served briefly as a literary agent, and toward the end of his life began offering extension courses in the writing of popular literature and television at the University of California, Los Angeles. They were well attended.

26

Beaumont was a people person: he loved interacting with others. His contemporaries report that he had a naturally happy disposition.

III.

NONFICTION WORKS

Paradoxically, just as Charles Beaumont had a fixation on death and illness, he also had a superhuman drive to savor all of the complex pursuits life had to offer, possessing a love for living life that was contagious to those around him. Faced with the terrifying knowledge of the fatal illness that was destroying him from the inside out, he chose to fight to the end rather than commit suicide. One night he peered into the bathroom mirror at his rapidly aging face with a razor held in each hand ready to slash his wrists. But he made a separate peace with himself, put the razors away, and went on fighting. For Beaumont, it was better to struggle than to acquiesce, better to fight than to whimper.

In examining Beaumont's life and his writings, we quickly realize that whatever he created he designed as a mirror reflection of some sacred part of himself. Each character creation displays a part of Beaumont the man, whether it is a female or a male character, and each experience in the story reflects the author's life experiences to one degree or another. Beaumont cannot be separated from his writings in an analytical study because both are interlocked, much in the fashion of a complex, two-thousand piece puzzle. A dynamic individual, Beaumont had two sides to his personality: he was a dreamer and a romantic, but he was a realist and a pragmatist. Both sides flowed together evenly in his writing.

Whether writing personality pieces, such as the one on actor Robert Mitchum, whom he greatly admired, or writing about jazz or nostalgia, it is apparent from studying these writings that Beaumont had an inquisitive, inquiring intellect. A jazz enthusiast, Beaumont used Louis Armstrong as a model for some of Spoof Collins's attributes in "Black Country" in perhaps what could be best described as a reverse manner; he created a person opposite to Armstrong while at the same time recalling Armstrong with fondness and admiration. In "Red Beans & Ricely Yours" (1955), Beaumont writes the story of Louis "Satchmo" Armstrong, who is remembered as one of jazz's greatest trumpeters. The article is both a biography of Armstrong while at the same providing a moving tribute to the black trumpeter and his contributions to jazz. It also reflects Beaumont's keen attachment to jazz music.

Of the numerous nonfictional works written under Beaumont's byline, the most impressive pieces were gathered together in the book, *Remember? Remember?* (1963). This collection of nostalgic articles concerning Americana includes such essays as: "Holiday Song," "The Little Fellow," "Tune in Yesterday," "And a Glass of Water, Please," "Don't Miss the Next Thrilling Chapter," "Who's Got the Funnies?," "The Bloody Pulps," "There's Nothing to Be Afraid of, My Child," "Good Lord, It's Alive!," "Who Closed the Castles?," "A Million Laughs," "The Undead," and "Lament for the High Iron."

"Holiday Song" recalls the wonders of holidays and what they mean, giving a poignant look at such days as Christmas, Halloween, and July the Fourth. That holidays have lost their magic in a technological society is the major point of this piece. The article provides a concise historical analysis of each day; for those readers interested in an unusual look at what the Saint Valentine's Day is really about, this is the place to investigate first. "The Little Fellow" examines Charlie Chaplin's success and fall from grace, focusing on Chaplin's life and movie career. Beaumont saw Chaplin's creations as representing the best of humankind—the spirit of humankind in baggy pants, walking unafraid into the unknown.

"Tune In Yesterday" is one of Beaumont's most complex articles, and it concerns America's love affair with radio programs before the advent of television. It is a look at a time when life was simpler and when people were more able to communicate with each other without fear. He discusses the many popular radio programs of the times, among them: *Jack Armstrong, the All-American Boy!*, *The Lone Ranger*, *I Love a Mystery*, *Little Orphan Annie*, *Amos and Andy*, *Buck Rogers*, *First Nighter*, *Gang Busters*, *Og, Son of Fire*, *The Shadow*, *Peter Quill*, *Captain Midnight*, *Inner Sanctum*, *The Green Hornet*, *The Hermit's Cave*, *The Molle Mystery Theatre*, *Suspense*, *The Goldbergs*, and *Stella Dallas*, among others. He credits Norman Corwin and Arch Oboler as being the two major dramatic writers for radio, without whose fine writing talents radio would not have been what it was for Americans tuning in nightly. *The Lone Ranger*, *I Love a Mystery*, *Inner Sanctum*, *Suspense*, and *Peter Quill* were among Beaumont's favorites.

"And a Glass of Water, Please" reflects Beaumont's fondness for the drugstore soda fountains of his youth, and the excitement of sitting at one of the wire-legged stools. "Don't Miss the Next Thrilling Chapter" is a look at the exciting movie serials of the '30s, '40s, and '50s, such as: *Daredevil Jack*, *Secret of the Submarine*, *The Diamond from the Sky*, *The Fighting Marine* (starring boxer Gene Tunney), and *The Master Mystery*, among others, and their appeal for the American public. Two important serials of the time were *The Last Frontier* (starring Lon Chaney, Jr.) and *The Valley of Vanishing Men* (starring Slim Summerville and Bill Elliot).

"Who's Got the Funnies?" is an intriguing, humorous look at newspaper comic strips, and the genuine enjoyment they give to people. Beaumont comments that Hitler loved *Mickey Mouse*, Mussolini loved *Popeye*, Emperor Hirohito loved *Blondie*, and Franklin Delano Roosevelt loved *Dick Tracy*—each leader took pleasure in these comic strip figures for different reasons. Beaumont gives a short history of the development of newspaper comics starting in 1895, and presents its continued development down to modern times. The comic strip is seen as an art form, not just a medium of entertainment, and Beaumont spends careful time and thought commenting on such classic strips as: *Krazy Kat*, *Smokey Stover*, *Alley Oop*, *Mandrake the Magician*, *Prince Valiant*, *Li'l Abner*, *Pogo*, *Peanuts*, and *Terry and the Pirates*, among others. Beaumont saw the comics as both enjoyable entertainment and as a true art form reflecting the cultural attributes of its time. It is important to note that Charles Beaumont also sold thirty scripts to Whitman Publications's Dell Comics line; ten of these were written in collaboration with William F. Nolan. Carrying no byline, they appeared in *Mickey Mouse Comics*, *Woody Woodpecker Comics*, *Walt Disney Comics*, *Tweety and Sylvester Comics*, and *Donald Duck Comics*. Not only did Beaumont enjoy comic strips and comic books, and see them as an important art form in their own right, he was diverse enough in his far-reaching interests to write scripts for them. In whatever field Beaumont wrote for, he was a visual writer with the innate ability to project images, and he could intuitively tap in on the wellspring of universal experience to make his images meaningful to all readers. This aspect of Beaumont's writing ability will ensure his literary reputation as a major American writer of the twentieth century. In addition to his masterpiece of prose fiction, *The Intruder*, he will be remembered for several stories and a handful of articles concerning interpretations of the American Dream.

"The Bloody Pulps" describes the mass-market fiction magazines published during the Depression years for the average American, including such publications as: *Doc Savage*, *The Spider*, *Black Mask*, *Marvel Tales*, *The Phantom*, and *Weird Tales*, among others. August Derleth is mentioned in the article, and there are insightful looks into such magazine character creations as Doc Savage and his crew, the Shadow, Frank Merriwell, Tom Edison, Jr., Nick Carter, Horatio Alger, Diamond Dick, Pawnee Bill, among others. Beaumont discusses other magazines and writers for the pulps, and there is a moving tribute to Frederick Schiller Faust, who wrote under the pen names of Max Brand, George Owen Baxter, Martin Dexter, Erin Evans, David Manning, Peter Dawson, John Frederick, and Pete Morland. Beaumont considered Faust one of the best writers of his time, and points out that he was a highly complex individual—a serious author concerned with serious literary themes. Faust was killed while serving as a reporter on the front lines in Italy during World War Two, without having achieved the literary recognition he right-fully deserved. Faust is best remembered today for the western novels he wrote under his pen name of Max Brand, which are still being exhumed from the pulps and published in book form. Beaumont says that the heyday of the pulps came to an end during 1950 and faded from the scene, becoming part of the American heritage.

"There's Nothing to Be Afraid of, My Child" is Beaumont's appraisal of amusement parks in the United States and how their thrills and terrors were replaced by Disneyland; in this article, he analyzes the theme of fear and terror found in the original parks and offers some insights as to why this theme was important to the average American seeking cheap thrills.

"Good Lord, It's Alive!" discusses the importance of the horror film in American movie-making, and the public's continued interest in such films over a period of decades. Beaumont cites the following such movies as the classics of the genre: *King Kong, Frankenstein, Dracula, Metropolis, The Day the Earth Stood Still, The Invasion of the Body Snatchers, The Cat People, The Werewolf of London*, and *The Cabinet of Doctor Caligari*, among others. Beaumont's favorite was *King Kong*; no matter how often he saw it, it always continued to fascinate and thrill him with its fresh approach to its subject.

"Who Closed the Castles?" is a look at the marvelous movie theaters of the thirties and forties and their demolition as unwanted relics from the past. "A Million Laughs" shows Beaumont looking at the need for laughter in everybody's life; he compares current comedy to the films of Mabel Normand, the Keystone Kops, Max Linder, Ben Turpin, Chester Conklin, Fatty Arbuckle, Charlie Chaplin, Mack Swain, Hank Mann, Al St. John, Charley Chase, Slim Summerville, Harold Lloyd, Buster Keaton, W. C. Fields, and Laurel and Hardy, among others. Beaumont considers the two greatest American clowns in comedy as Danny Kaye and Red Skelton.

"The Undead" tells of Beaumont's meeting with actor Bela Lugosi during the Spring of 1952; it is a sensitive portrayal of Lugosi the actor and human being. The loneliness of the old star in Hollywood prior to his death is made painfully clear. At the time of their meeting, Beaumont had created a screen story as a vehicle to bring Lugosi back to motion pictures; unfortunately, due to lack of interest in Lugosi and a movie starring him, the project was never funded. "Lament for the High Iron" concerns the time in America's past when locomotives and railroads were foremost in the American imagination as an exciting mode of travel.

Charles Beaumont was a prolific writer, and penned many articles and columns for vastly different publications. Some of these appeared in *The Magazine of Fantasy & Science Fiction* during the 1950s. In "The Seeing I" (*The Magazine of Fantasy & Science Fiction*, December, 1959), he discusses the importance of Rod Serling's television series, *The Twilight Zone*, and makes the prophetic forecast that Serling's dramatic series would be an innovator for dramatic form in the television media. In his column "The Science Screen" for *Fantasy & Science Fiction*, he reviews then-current movies—their merits, their strengths, their weaknesses, the state of the art—and some of his best columns appeared on the following dates: December, 1955; June, 1956; September, 1956; and, June, 1957.

An avid sports car racer, Beaumont also wrote many articles for the racing magazines on this subject, some of which were later reprinted in book form. One of his best pieces in this genre is the autobiographical fiction story called "Man to Beat," which is the suspenseful account of a professional sports car racer, examining why he likes to race.

IV.

TELEVISION SCRIPTS

As a television script writer, Beaumont's work shows his skill in handling dialogue and societal themes, and creating suspenseful situations. The author was tremendously prolific as a script writer, and some of his teleplays were adapted from his own earlier published stories.

Charles Beaumont's first script was "Masquerade," written during 1954 for *Four Star Playhouse*; it was not until 1957 that he became more active in this medium. Initially, Beaumont collaborated on teleplays for such programs as: *Wanted: Dead or Alive*, with George Clayton Johnson; *Have Gun, Will Travel*, with Richard Matheson; *One Step Beyond* and *Naked City*, with William F. Nolan; *Cheyenne, Richard Diamond*, and *Route 66*, with John Tomerlin; *Thriller*, with OCee Ritch, and *Alfred Hitchcock Presents*, with Jerry Sohl, among many others.

As a television writer, Beaumont's most lasting contribution and the reason why he is primarily remembered today, is for his brilliant teleplays for Rod Serling's landmark TV series, *The Twilight Zone*. The reader will easily recall the best of these scripts, including such classic episodes as: "Perchance to Dream" (Richard Conte played the role of Edward Hall); "Elegy" (Cecil Kellaway played the role of Jeremy Wickwire); "Long Live Walter Jameson" (Kevin McCarthy played the role of Professor Walter Jameson); "A Nice Place to Visit" (Larry Blyden played the role of Rocky Valentine); "The Howling Man" (John Carradine played the role of Brother Jerome); "Shadow Play" (Dennis Weaver played the role of Adam Grant); "The Jungle" (John Dehner played the role of Alan Richards); "In His Image" (George Grizzard played the roles of Talbot and Ryder); "Passage on the *Lady Ann*" (Lee Philips played the role of Allan Ransome); "Printer's Devil" (Burgess Meredith played the role of Mr. Smith), and "Miniature" (Robert Duvall played the role of Charley), among many others.

V.

MOTION PICTURE SCREENPLAYS

Charles Beaumont loved the movies. He wrote or was directly involved with nine movie screenplays during his lifetime that were actually produced. One of the finest and most sensitive and humorous of his scripts is *The Seven Faces of Dr. Lao*. Movie critics and movie fans will note their own favorites from the listing that follows. Each film includes Beaumont's creative and sensitive dialogue:

Queen of Outer Space, a science fiction flick starring Zsa Zsa Gabor which appeared in 1958, is one of the author's least efforts; an expedition lands on Venus, which is ruled entirely by women. *The Intruder*, based on Beaumont's novel of the same name, appeared in 1962, being directed by Roger Corman; the author played the role of high school principal Harley Paton in the movie which starred the talented young actor, William Shatner, later to become better known for his role as Captain Kirk on the *Star Trek* TV series.

The Wonderful World of the Brothers Grimm, adapted from the Grimm Brothers' children's folktales, was produced in 1962; Beaumont collaborated on the screenplay with William Roberts and David Harmon. *Burn, Witch, Burn*, adapted from Fritz Leiber's classic novel, *Conjure Wife*, appeared during 1962; Beaumont collaborated on the screenplay with Richard Matheson. *The Premature Burial*, loosely adapted from the classic Poe tale of horror, was released during 1962; Beaumont collaborated on the screenplay with Ray Russell.

The Haunted Palace, based on H. P. Lovecraft's classic, *The Strange Case of Charles Dexter Ward*, appeared during 1963. *The Seven Faces of Dr. Lao* starred Tony Randall, being released during 1964; it was adapted from Charles G. Finney's well-known fantasy novel, *The Circus of Dr. Lao*.

Masque of the Red Death, another adaptation of a Poe story, appeared during 1964, and Beaumont shared screenplay credit with R. Wright Campbell, who later became better known as a mystery writer. *Mister Moses*, released in 1965 and adapted from the novel by Max Catto, starred Robert Mitchum, who leads an African tribe to its new homeland. This was the last movie work to appear by Charles Beaumont during his lifetime, and screenplay credit on this movie was shared with Monja Danischevsky.

A previously unproduced screenplay, *Brain Dead*, was adapted by Adam Simon and released in 1990. This science fiction horror film uses the dreams-with-nightmare theme to terrify its audiences.

VI.

THE INTRUDER (1959)

A mainstream novel dealing with racism and power struggle, Charles Beaumont's *The Intruder* is, as many critics stated upon its publication during 1959, one of the finest novels published during that year. A complex work, it shows Beaumont at his best. It is Beaumont's longest novel, and it reveals his ability to create believable characters, construct intricate imagery, delineate social themes, and write tense, dramatic dialogue within the structural form of a novel. *The Intruder* clearly illustrates that had Beaumont lived and pursued his dream of writing novels, he would have become a major novelist in modern American literature.

When Christopher Marlowe (1564-1593) wrote his play, *The Tragicall History of Dr. Faustus*, he created a work which was completely dominated by a single character whose dynamic, unrelenting force of personality gave intense unity to the play. Charles Beaumont achieved a similar feat with his central character of *The Intruder*, Adam Cramer. In the case of Cramer—the stranger and outsider who arrives in the small, sleepy Southern town of Claxton—he is depicted as a man possessed by an overriding passion for power; and if the proverbial Devil may be identified, it is in the person of Cramer's helpmate and professor, Dr. Max Blake. The means through which Cramer seeks power is via the Society of National American Patriots (SNAP), an organization eerily reminiscent of the far rightwing groups so prevalent today. As a base for the Society, Claxton will serve as Cramer's starting point to consolidate his power. The Faustian figure has been a prevalent literary theme ever since the historical Faust lived in the fifteenth century. However, just as Thomas Mann did

did not deal directly with the Faust legend in his *Doktor Faustus*, but used it as a parallel to the fall of his own character, Adrian Leverkuhn, Charles Beaumont performs a similar literary accomplishment in the handling of his character, Adam Cramer. Beaumont's fictional creation is a modern day American Faustus in love with and possessed by power for the sake of power. He becomes a dark, shadowy force in the flesh as he pursues his goals.

Adam Cramer is depicted by the author as a masculine, sensually handsome man with straight, dark brown hair, blue eyes, a slightly bent nose and thick lips. He has a firm handshake, looks directly in the face of the person with whom he is conversing, and successfully projects a societal mask of warmth and friendliness coupled with a pleasant voice. Blessed with a charismatic nature, he employs it to guide those with whom he comes in contact towards evil, to achieve his goal of power, and to influence those around him; for him the ends always justify the means. An Americanized version of the Byronic hero, Adam Cramer is the twentieth century Everyman perverted by a lust for power.

In the early chapters of the novel, Cramer arrives at Claxton and establishes his residence at the Union Hotel; he describes himself as a special sort of social worker come to aid Claxton with its "integration problem." Later, he identifies himself as being from Los Angeles, California and a representative of SNAP. The early chapters of the novel establish character identities and individual societal roles, a process that builds throughout the course of the plot, each section and person fitting together like neat, precise brickwork until the individual is captured fully in his or her essence. Beaumont is equally at ease in handling female or male characters, making all of his individuals of both sexes real and believable to the reader.

Early in the plot, the sociological theme of paradoxical perception becomes apparent: what you see may in reality be not what you thought you saw at all, for often the shadow cast is more of a reality than the figure which cast it. This is personified in the character of Adam Cramer as he interacts with those around him and wears the appropriate societal mask he needs to meet the requirements of each confrontation. Although the literary theme of masques—a form of entertainment prevalent among English aristocracy during the sixteenth and seventeenth centuries—is evident in *The Intruder*, Beaumont's treatment of it is completely Americanized and sociological in design. What was once a masque becomes a societal mask, and the societal role is interpreted accordingly; societal roles in contemporary technological societies are more complex and different than they were in the sociophilosophical setting of the pre-industrial age. To a sociologist studying the processes of masque entertainment, it has its origins in primitive fertility rites; its development towards complexity comes through the demands of the civilizing process upon cultures.

Those interested in how the masque form of entertainment developed from primitive fertility rites through its height of popularity during the 1600s, should delve into primitive magic and religion, and then glance at some of the work written by Ben Jonson, Inigo Jones, Thomas Middleton, George Chapman, John Fletcher, and Francis Beaumont. "The Woman Hater and the Knight of the Burning Pestle" by Francis Beaumont (1584-1616) and "The Masque of Beauty," "The Masque of Queens," and "Oberon, the Faery Prince" by Ben Jonson (1573-1637) are excellent examples of the masque theme in dramatic form. *Peg Woffington*, a novel written by Charles Reade (1814-1884), is another exemplar of this genre.

Societal mask and societal role in contemporary America are schizoid by necessity; high tech societal settings require a schizophrenic thinking approach, especially from an ethics perspective, for without the individual having the ease to change masks and roles at any given moment in time, he or she cannot survive. One mask and one role no longer applies today: there must be many. When an individual is locked in to a particular goal or dream, and must accomplish it or perish, an open mask may be worn to fit any role demanded at a given time; however, in this instance beneath that particular mask is usually found the naked face of violence. The naked face of violence is

40

painfully and horrifyingly intense in *The Intruder*'s characters, Bart Carey and Phil Dongen.

From a philosophical viewpoint, Adam Cramer is the Americanized descendant of Niccolò di Bernardo Machiavelli (1469-1527), invested with an ethical set of values borrowed from Friedrich Wilhelm Nietzsche (1844-1900). Cramer exists in a sensate cultural mentality, and he fits in perfectly with the sociophilosophical concept of the twentieth century sensate system developed by American sociologist Pitirim Sorokin: a sensate cultural setting is based on the idea that the material world is the one we experience with our senses, and exist and function in; what we experience in this material world is the only reality there is, and transcendent reality is denied. Material goals are the only reality worth achieving.

In Cramer's case, his oftentimes cynical sensate approach to life is expressed in his pursuit of sensate goals, which he justifies and uses to influence others to justify in terms of ideational rationalizations based on a transcendent value system that is mere window dressing. In a power struggle situation, whatever the prevalent transcendent value system is, this system must be utilized in any way possible to make the struggle seem noble and respectful for the individual or individuals seeking to gain control of power. And what is deviance in one circle may not be considered deviance in another; those in power define what is normal and what is considered deviant. If Cramer defines something that is evil as good, or vice versa, and has the power to enforce that definition of the situation, then it becomes such. Absolute power means absolute control over all definitions of the situation.

In an involved dialogue between Cramer and Verne Shipman, Cramer is seen as a most adroit individual in societal masking as he actively seeks to gain control of the situation with Shipman; he will wear whatever societal mask is necessary to ensure Shipman's loyalty. He appeals to Shipman's better judgment in stopping desegregation, insisting that Claxton could serve as a rallying point for concerned whites who do not want blacks and other bad racial types moving in and taking over. Shipman is a logical starting point for Cramer, because Shipman has money and belongs to the upper class of Claxton. In very convincing words, Cramer states that desegregation will lead to the mongrelization of the entire white race in the United States. By the end of the chapter, Cramer has convinced Shipman that Shipman will play a key role in whatever happens; he departs, leaving Shipman with a paper titled, "Integration of Negroes with Whites Unconstitutional." What the Supreme Court has recently ruled, Cramer will attempt to destroy; integration and desegregation must be thwarted. As the plot unfolds, Cramer is eventually able to recruit many townspeople to his cause and to stir up race hatred. Cramer's speech-making ability is remarkable in the way in which he can stir and activate long-buried emotions, and although his words are those of a concerned bigot, he illuminates the whole, unhealthy side of what racial hatred is really about. Historically, the universality of what Cramer says exemplifies the best attributes of a gifted speaker in search of power and a scapegoat.

Harley Paton, the high school principal, stands in Cramer's way. He represents loyalty to the law, and if desegregation and equality mean precisely that, then it is his obligation to see that the law is carried out and his school became integrated. In a tense encounter with Cramer and others, Paton states simply and with courage that although he may not personally support integration of the races, he does support law and order. It is a stall, for later Paton confides in the English teacher, Miss Angoff, that he does indeed support integration and that it has been a lifelong dream of his to see true equality. But to admit this would mean his removal from a position of power, and without the position he would be unable to help the movement. Pleased at his response, Agnes Angoff leaves: she thinks of Harley Paton as one of the many faces of courage. The idea of courage as a societal mask is voiced, and the effects of peer pressure are visualized.

Cramer does manage to seduce the high school girl, Ella McDaniel, who is sixteen-years-old. There are flashback scenes to Cramer's past, and the reader sees him as a young man struggling to control his strong sexuality. In a long letter to Max Blake, Cramer reveals he feels at home in his role as a rabble-rouser for the cause, and looks forward to gaining more support and even more power. Later, it is with great pleasure that he watches as a cross is burned; he is gaining control over the townspeople that can assist him. As the book progresses, Beaumont at times uses the Faulknerian technique of flashback. Chapter Seventeen concerns Cramer's mother, and through her, the reader is able to see what kind of childhood and background Adam came from; from the psychoanalytical perspective, it gives an interesting analysis on the Mother-Son relationship in contemporary America. To understand some of the reasons Adam Cramer behaves as he does is to also understand his mother; to understand both is to gain insight into the dark side of parental social bonds, self-hatred, and the looking-glass self.

American sociologist Charles Horton Cooley's theory of the looking-glass self manifests itself at different times in the novel, and it is important when understanding Cramer's formation of self; for in defining a sense of personal identity, the self is the image the child develops of himself only by finding out what other people think of him. To do this, the child uses other individuals as a mirror to discover what he is actually like. The looking-glass self does not stop at childhood, but continues throughout adulthood in one guise or another, depending upon the social circumstances of the individual involved. Prescriptions—things one must do societally, and proscriptions—things one must not do societally, can be transposed by the effect of prejudice projection—placing traits on others that the individual cannot admit to having himself. Failure is frowned upon in the United States, but success is favored; if success implies failure in those less fortunate than yourself, and you possess the ability to enforce that particular definition of the situation, what better way for Adam Cramer to remain an enduring success than to gain power over the townspeople who in turn have power over the blacks. Territoriality is achieved, while the element of failure is displaced.

Cramer's relationship with Sam's wife, Vy Griffin, is a study in role conflict, role loss, and role tolerance. In Chapter Twenty-Two, Sam confronts Cramer concerning the affair between Cramer and Vy, and during the process of the dialogue, the reader sees the chinks in Cramer's armor, even though Cramer is not fully aware of them yet. Even at this late stage, Cramer cannot admit to internal weaknesses that would betray his lust for power and his plans for the consolidation of his power. He refuses to contemplate that he may himself become the final scapegoat. Cramer is caught between the fantasy of what he wants existence to be, and the logic of what it can become due to his own errors.

In Chapter Twenty-Three, Tom McDaniel, the editor of the *Messenger* and father of Ella, is maimed by a mob led by Reverend Lorenzo Niesen and Bart Carey. Violence has revealed its naked face in the townspeople. In Chapter Twenty-Four, in a brilliant narrative of political, social, and philosophical confrontation, Cramer encounters his professor, Dr. Max Blake and is told that he is no longer needed and that his role in Blake's scheme is finished. Cramer survives the tense confrontation, gains a sense of spiritual strength, and replaces his professor as a power figure.

With Ella McDaniel's help, Cramer plans to regain full control of the situation following the brutal attack on her father, Tom; he convinces her to frame the black high school student, Joey Green, for rape. But Harley Paton senses a trap, and he tells Miss Angoff that he doubted the attempted rape by Joey Green ever took place; and, when a mob starts to form, he seeks to protect Joey Green, who is then attending school. In a moving scene, the reader sees the two—Paton the White Man and Green the Black Man—as everyday human beings caught in a situation that neither one of them made—or wanted. In a surprise move, Joey Green decides to face the mob and declare his innocence of the rape accusation. Refusing to believe him, the mob takes Green, and Paton is forcefully restrained from aiding his student by the psychotic Abner West. The mob is stopped by the surprise visit of Sam Griffin. He has

44

gotten a confession from Ella, and she confesses that Adam
Cramer had put her up to everything. Cramer denies this
and in the process discredits himself before the mob; Joey
Green is set free, and the mob disperses, leaving Cramer
finally alone with his illusions. Loneliness is all that
Cramer has left.

In the closing scenes of the novel, Sam Griffin and
Adam Cramer confront each other for the last time. Griffin
slaps Cramer hard twice. The mob disappears, and Cramer
realizes that his dream of power is shattered forever.

The novel concludes as Griffin drops bullets at
Cramer's feet; the bullets came from Cramer's revolver
which he no longer possesses. Adam watches until the man
is gone; he does not move, but stands there thinking of his
lost role as a power figure. Adam Cramer—the first Adam
in a small Southern Eden—has been devoured by his own
serpent; he is dead in more ways than one, and the bullets
on the ground merely tell him that he does not need a revolver to finish a suicide already committed by himself.
The essence of Adam Cramer is dead, and only the physical
husk remains. The rite of passage is over. Sociologically,
the rite of passage is any ceremony that marks or designates
an individual's moving on to a newer or higher stage of social acceptance; for Adam Cramer, destroyed by his own
perverted lust for societal power, the only stage left for him
to reach is the one left to him by his peers: death.

The Intruder is a complex novel. Had Charles
Beaumont pursued his dream of writing fiction rather than
remaining in the television and movie entertainment world
as a gifted script and screenwriter, he would have left a
major legacy to modern American literature. As a novelist,
Beaumont had the potential for becoming the equal with
John Steinbeck and Saul Bellow, given his creativity, perspective on life, and vision of the American Dream in all of
its terrifying complexity. As it is, he left behind only two
long fictions: *The Intruder*, and *Run from the Hunter*.

VII.

RUN FROM THE HUNTER (1957)

Run from the Hunter, Beaumont's first novel, was written with his friend John Tomerlin under the joint pseudonym, Keith Grantland, and published by Fawcett Gold Medal Books as part of their long series of original paperback hardboiled mystery and suspense novels. *Hunter* actually comes closer to being mainstream fiction than a mystery novel, with its emphasis on internal and external desires of characters in conflict and societal role. It is reminiscent of certain works by Italo Svevo (1861-1928), Horace Walpole (1717-1797), Romain Rolland (1866-1944), Alphonse Daudet (1840-1897), and Thomas Mann (1875-1955). This short novel also reveals Charles Beaumont's skills as a master of dramatic dialogue and suspenseful action.

Run from the Hunter is the story of Christopher Adams, a newspaper reporter caught in an intrigue of murder and masquerade during Mardi Gras at New Orleans, Louisiana. Mardi Gras, originally a French celebration of the last day of pre-Lenten carnival in imitation of a Roman sacrificial procession, serves to set the theme of death and societal conflict in Beaumont's schema. The setting is sensate America, and the social atmosphere is materialistic.

The novel opens with Adams on his way to the Alabama State Penitentiary; a muscular, medium-built man, he sits in a reflective manner as the journey progresses. He is accompanied by Frank Giorgio, kingpin of Alabama gambling and a convicted murderer, and a female narcotics pusher. Adams has been sentenced for the murder of a socialite named Steffany Fontaine—a crime he did not commit. Giorgio tells Adams he knows that he is innocent, and that he will help him clear his name if Adams helps him es-

46

cape the train they are riding on when the pre-arranged wreck occurs. Adams refuses, but the "accident" does take place despite his efforts to alert the policeman, Brewer. Giorgio is killed in the wreckage by a train wheel. Adams makes his escape into the swamp, eventually discovering a road. Adams's thoughts give the reader an intriguing glance at the man's background. Beaumont is proficient in the way he utilizes this literary technique, and he enjoys letting the reader see inside his character's mind.

In Chapter Two, the reader is introduced to the man responsible for Adams's arrest: Police Lieutenant Howard Carr. Carr tells his wife that he has been contacted by authorities about the train derailment and Adams's escape into the swamp; he informs her he must personally handle the matter, and reveals himself as a hardnosed cop who does not let any job he undertakes remain unfinished. In the meantime, Adams stumbles into what he perceived as a deserted cabin, but discovers that it is the home of a woman and her twenty-year-old daughter, Loni Gaillard. His wounds from the train wreck are doctored, and he is given shelter for the night; both Edna Mae and her daughter, Loni, know who the man is from the newspaper accounts of the murder. Beaumont gives the reader an in-depth character analysis of both women, revealing that both have known good and bad times but have retained their basic humanity and kindness. Adams drifts off to sleep, knowing that the hunters are after him.

An idea that appears in this section is one of an ethical nature, stemming from both Ancient Greek and Asian philosophy: if one cannot trust the kindness of strangers, then who can one trust? Adams has placed his safety in the hands of the women. The totem—an object oftentimes used as a symbol of an important emotion or idea—appears in this chapter as the rifle with which Loni uses to threaten Adams; it turns out to be unloaded, yet the message is vividly clear. The rifle represents both death and violence; in the case of *The Intruder* as well as in this novel, the weapons of death and violence are everywhere evident. Violence requires a high degree of emotionalism to sustain successfully, and a weapon accompanying such activities—whether used or not used—is the handmaiden of violence in whatever guise it presents itself.

Chapter Three relates the details of Adams's war days and his dream of become a playwright after he returned from service, something he never achieved. While admiring the body of Loni Galliard, Adams recalls Steffany Fontaine and other flames from his past, and his strong sexual nature is revealed to the reader. Adams tells Edna Mae about the murder, stating he did not commit the crime; his conviction was based entirely on circumstantial evidence. While preparing to leave, he is stopped by the sound of approaching automobiles. He escapes with the aid of the two women and starts his search for the real murderer. Through Chapter Seven the plot continues to become more complex, and the societal roles of Beaumont's characters become solidly delineated and much more clear: the sociological theme of paradoxical perception is at work, with nobody knowing for sure what is what is really happening and what is illusionary. Several societal masks dissolve, revealing the true natures of the persons behind the masks.

By the end of Chapter Nine, Adams and Loni have become completely enmeshed in the tangle of clues leading to the real murderer, and they have also become greatly attached to each other. They discover a packet of narcotics linked to the murders. The Chapter concludes as they make love. Loni is seen as a strong, willful woman with a mind of her own, an individual wholly unafraid of making difficult decisions: she is an equal match for Adams. In a subtle sense, Adams and Loni are mirror images of each other.

Chapter Ten finds the Mardi Gras celebration falling towards the characters like a hungry shadow in search of a sacrifice to satisfy its bloodlust. As one clue leads to another, key figures in the murder of Steffany Fontaine begin turning up dead. Chapters Eleven and Twelve find Adams and Loni coming close to the real murderer after an unexpected and revealing confrontation with the drug runner, Sid Simpson; suddenly confronted with the possibility of their own deaths, they manage to escape on Simpson's cabin cruiser. With Loni safe, Adams later seeks out the murderer by himself; he is appropriately dressed in a masquerade costume of a pirate. In Chapter Thirteen, Adams unveils and confronts the murderer: Sheridan Paige. Chapter Fourteen explains why the murder happened, and Paige's love and hate for the beautiful Steffany: blackmail and narcotics are secondary to what Paige had felt for Steffany. In an ironic sense, his murder of her was part of the American Dream, the constant striving for Success—if he could not reach her own social standing, then he would bring her down to his, and failing this, he had to eliminate her to survive as a man.

Each character in this novel is in pursuit, directly or indirectly, of some aspect of the American Dream. Different goals require different approaches for successfully reaching those goals; failure to achieve success is a failure of one's person. Beaumont's subtle attack upon the idea of the American Dream and the nightmarish societal masks it sometimes forces Americans to wear as they pursue it, is but one aspect of this novel. Crowds and crowd scenes are used to display the loneliness of the outsider, whether that outsider is running from some danger (running from the hunter), or simply just another lonely face in the crowd. That Paige is nearly insane is clear from Adams's comment on the way the man stares at him while he converses; that Paige will go on killing—no matter how many people it takes to secure his freedom and identity—is further evidence of his own madness and that of society at large. A brief struggle ensues, and Paige escapes from Adams.

The final chapter, Fifteen, has Adams reversing roles and pursuing the fleeing murderer. Paige, the newspaper columnist who monitored and reported on the affairs of the wealthy upper class, and at the same time served their interests, now finds that he must kill Adams to protect his role. When the police arrive, he refuses to acknowledge that the masquerade is over and that he has been unmasked as the true murderer. The police open fire on the suspect, and Paige falls into the water, only to be crushed to death by a boat slamming him into the pilings. The society reporter disappears beneath the water; his body will be recovered later. No longer running from the hunter and free to pursue his own life once again, Adams rejoins his beloved Loni, and the novel ends with a new beginning, the chance for the lovers to plan a life together.

In his first published novel, Charles Beaumont demonstrates all of the hallmarks of his future writings: a love for language, the mix of tense societal situations leading to an explosion of rage, in-depth character analyses, the use of vivid imagery, dramatic dialogue, sensitivity, a keen sense for social commentary coupled with an eclectic style, and a vivid visual imagination. Loneliness, the pursuit of a dream, and death will remain key themes in his work throughout the rest of his short career.

VIII.

THE SHORT FICTION

Charles Beaumont began writing short stories in the late 1940s, and quickly made his first sales to the science fiction pulps and genre magazines, graduating to *Playboy* and the other higher-paying slicks when those markets arrived in the mid-1950s. His production of short fiction had virtually ceased by 1960, when he moved into the more lucrative television market. Each of the stories has been covered in the order in which they were published, with comprehensive plot summaries and some small attempt at analysis. The *Selected Stories* included five previously unpublished pieces which are grouped at the end of this section.

Although most of Beaumont's short fiction could be considered SF, fantasy, or horror, he also wrote several significant mainstream stories and novellas, and a few pieces in other genres. All are listed below.

"The Devil, You Say?" (1951)

Narrated by a newspaperman named Ed, this is the story of Dick Lewis's encounter with the Devil himself. Lewis tells his story to his newspaper friends in a bar. Lewis, who inherited his father Elmer's newspaper, *The Danville Daily Courier*, is on the point of financial ruin when Satan appears—the Devil calls himself Mr. Jones. Mr. Jones guarantees the success of the newspaper, and before Dick can blink an eye, money is pouring in for new subscriptions. Along the way, Lewis encounters the lovely Elissa Traskers, and together, they attempt to displace the Devil. Lewis uses his typewriter to convey a message to

51

Mr. Jones's special press that the Devil has disappeared and so has the newspaper. Suddenly, Lewis discovers he is now a major columnist for the *New York Mirror*, and although Elissa is employed there, too, she recalls nothing of what has transpired and has no interest in Lewis. Lewis concludes his strange tale to Ed and the others with the promise that he is leaving journalism forever—which he does—and is greeted with mock sympathy and laughter. It is only at the conclusion of the story that Ed believes Lewis is telling the truth when he happens to see Mr. Jones leaning against the bar winking at him. Ed does not waste time in leaving the bar and going home.

Although this story is Beaumont's first published fiction, it is important for establishing the dream and death motifs as major themes in the author's work. Lewis gains his materialistic dream in a sensate culture by buying fame and making a deal that ensures his newspaper will make money (in other words, be successful); the cost is irrelevant, even if it means paying dues to Mr. Jones and ultimately winding up in hell if he makes the wrong moves. Essentially a study on the price of greed, "The Devil, You Say?" reflects Beaumont's interest in the idea that oftentimes a dream has more validity and more reality than faith in something or someone else. Faith is secondary to the dream. Faith can assist in fulfilling the dream, but faith can never take the place of the dream.

"The Beautiful People" (1952)

In this story the reader is confronted with a young woman named Mary Cuberle who does not want or desire to undergo a transformation that will make her essentially like everyone else. In a sensate society that demands conformity and sameness, there is no room for individuality and pursuit of personal dreams. The transformation means the death of Mary's psyche. At the close of the story, following an involved dialogue with the transformed, beautiful people in power, Mary sadly realizes she cannot retain her individuality, and is forced to undergo transformation to maintain order within the societal structure. She is strapped naked to a table; spread-eagled, she watches in horror as the machine descends, and she screams out the question that reflects her innermost fear: "when the transformation is completed, where will I find me!" This query symbolizes the core of her being, her soul, and her identity, now lost forever in a misty, colorful world of beautiful sameness and conformity.

This is a disturbing story, for Beaumont presents the reader with a view of what can happen as a result of behavior modification and Skinnerism carried to its logical extreme, before such techniques became fashionable. The stories also touches on the idea of selfhood. Sociologist George Herbert Mead saw the importance of selfhood, dual perspective, and the "I" and the "me" in the individual's life and the individual's manner of making meaningful choices. By destroying the selfhood of the individual, as well as the attributes of dual perspective and the "I" and the "me," the will of the individual is also eliminated. This is the goal of conformity, for conformity eliminates the need for creative individuality.

"Elegy" (1953)

"Elegy" was one of Charles Beaumont's favorite fantasy creations. It appeared in 1953, and later was converted by Beaumont into a teleplay of the same name for *The Twilight Zone* television series, being first televised on February 19, 1960. It is the story of three space travelers—Meyers, Webber, and Kirby—looking for home.

Low on fuel, their space craft lands on an asteroid which resembles Earth, but nothing is quite the same there. They are greeted by the caretaker of the place, Jeremy Wickwire, who informs them they have landed on an exclusive cemetery where the dead are permitted to realize their greatest wish in life after they are dead. The three earthlings say their greatest wish and dream is to be on their space craft headed home.

Too late, the three men realize that the android Wickwire has poisoned their drinks, and they die. Wickwire places the embalmed figures of the three men in their space craft and insures the continued peace and solitude of the cemetery known as Happy Glades. A rather morbid story, even for Beaumont, "Elegy" was rewritten for *The Twilight Zone*, making the character of Wickwire somewhat more gentle and humane. However, the basic themes of the story—pursuit of a dream, loneliness, and death—are vividly captured in the television version, and it remains one of the more popular *Twilight Zone* episodes.

"Elegy" as story and as television production illustrates Beaumont's concern with societal role and the definition of role, which is displayed here from both the perspectives of society and the individual, clearly showing how each interacts with the other.

"Fritzchen" (1953)

"Fritzchen" paints a devastating portrait of an American nuclear family: Jake and Edna Peldo and their eight-year-old son, Luther. Luther discovers an unusual creature near the seashore which he calls Fritzchen, and to his sadness, it is instantly confiscated for his father's pet shop. Put in a cage, it sobs with sounds like that of a drowning kitten; in appearance, it is a cross between a whale and a horsefly. During the time of Fritzchen's captivity the relationship between father and son continues to deteriorate. Jake sees Fritzchen as a solution to his dream of wealth and escape, but Luther sets fire to the creature, thus destroying both it and his father's dreams. Luther achieves his revenge against his father, while the father is trapped again in his sordid world. In a surprising ending, the cries of a human child, Luther, go unanswered, but the cries of the dying child, Fritzchen, are answered.

The giant nightmare of a creature that is Fritzchen's mother storms into the Peldo Pet Shop to answer the cries of her lost infant only to find that humans have burned it with fire. Her revenge promises to be swift and deadly.

54

"Fritzchen" is a complex story with Jungian overtones. Jake and Edna seem to regard Luther as a doll or a plaything; they perceive their existence in terms terms: of things to possess and to hold when valuable, and things easily discarded when no longer useful.

Beaumont correctly forecasts a time when American children will be perceived as worthless, that greed for materialistic things in a sensate American culture will displace the simple, uncomplex love of a parent for a child. Feelings of family love have degenerated in this story to mere vocalization—verbal masturbation and the nostalgic memories of the way Americans once lived and felt.

"The Last Caper" (1954)

Filled with vivid descriptions, colorful comparisons, and a strange brew of extraterrestrials, "The Last Caper" features one of Beaumont's most unusual plots while utilizing the techniques of irony and satire in a humorous vein. This is the story of Bartholomew Cornblossom and his search for the Chocolate Maltese Falcon. Bart is a private detective hired by a woman to retrieve this treasured family heirloom, and his search immediately places him in conflict with Mike Mallet. He assaults Mallet, then makes passionate love to Mallet's secretary. After wrecking Mallet's office, Bart still has no clue as to where to find the Falcon.

At one point Bart is mistaken for Gunther Awl, and is subjected to a broadcast of a soap opera as a form of torture; he cannot stand the trite dialogue he hears on the tube and agrees to confess everything, although he knows nothing. Bart then learns that the Chocolate Maltese Falcon is not what it appears to be, but instead it cleverly disguises the grains from a secret government explosive, identified as D-plus-4-over-X; the unstable substance is ready to explode and is potent enough to destroy an entire planet. Along the way there is much mayhem, and Mallet is killed along with a Venusian, a Martian, and a Jovian. It is only in death that the masks of the extraterrestrials are removed

55

and they are seen as they really appear to be; in death, the mask is gone and so is the pretense. Bart discovers to his dismay that the Chocolate Maltese Falcon was melted down into candy bars, which he has eaten.

Finally, Bartholomew Cornblossom explodes, in the end thinking that death is not so bad after all, for there are worse things that can befall a man while living an earthly existence. "The Last Caper" is woven around the theme of death, and serves as an intriguing study in societal interaction, role conflict, and paradoxical perception.

"Black Country" (1954)

Considered one of Charles Beaumont's finest short stories, "Black Country" captures the essence of African-American jazz and Black societal role in American culture. This poignant story serves as a complex, subtle analysis of societal role. Rich in texture, metaphor, simile, and imagery—trademarks of Beaumont's writing—"Black Country" traces the life of a jazz musician named Spoof Collins.

As a would-be actor, Beaumont realized the importance of spoken lines in establishing a character's identity, and knew that the societal role of the character would flesh out the spoken lines if both spoken lines and role were gracefully choreographed in a sensitive style. In a way Beaumont's greatest professional triumph as an actor came through his creation of memorable characters in his fiction. The life and vitality Beaumont could have given as a performer in movies or on stage was instead channeled into his fictional creations, investing them with a depth and reality that is often found lacking in current literature. Hollywood's loss is American literature's gain.

Beaumont gives careful attention to gender role, role conflict, role engulfment, role performance, role set, role strain, and role socialization in "Black Country." The characters are finely crafted and set like so many precious diamonds in a platinum wedding ring, each character interacting with and complementing the others in perfect harmony.

56

The story opens with Spoof Collins's burial by his friends; his earthly possessions have been placed by his side. His horn is lodged in his hands, positioned for play; his music is placed beside his body. He is lowered into the cemetery plot as his friends perform one of his musical compositions called *The Jimjam Man*. Darkness comes as the musicians play a round of Spoof Collins's songs, covering both them and the man with the trumpet who lays beneath them in the cold ground. It is the perfect setting for the beginning of a medieval mystery play with black and white players in a Black American cultural environment. Rose-Ann McHugh sings a song about the Black Country, and although it is a dirge about death, it also connects the African American man's role in life with the blackness of death. Sonny Holmes, Spoof's white friend in the Collins and His Crew jazz group, joins the serenade to his deceased black friend by playing on a new trumpet. It is a lonely scene.

As this shadow play story continues, the life of Spoof Collins unfolds; the roles of the other characters in his unusual life are interwoven into his existence and performed. Spoof is The Ol' Massuh of their lives. A bizarre relationship develops between Spoof, Rose-Ann, and Sonny; Spoof decides to write down all of his musical compositions.

Spoof knows time is rapidly running out for him, and his playing begins to deteriorate; one night he goes to his hotel room and commits suicide with a revolver. Later, the others find out Spoof was dying of cancer; rather than allow the disease to consume him, he acts to short-circuit its victory and calls the shot on his own death, picking his own time and place. The jazz group is reorganized and continues to perform and record under the new name, Sonny Holmes and His Crew.

Success follows Sonny now, like it did Spoof, and the story continues as the memory of Spoof lingers with the group long after the funeral; Sonny begins to take on the musical characteristics of Spoof and breaks off his relationship with Rose-Ann, the group's singer. In a poignant scene at the conclusion of the story, Sonny finds himself on the stage playing Spoof's trumpet and interpreting Spoof's musical visions; at last, Sonny is able to put out the kind of sound he has always dreamed of—a black musical sound that no white man can ever create. The story ends as the group performs Spoof's musical composition, *Black Country*, as a living tribute and appreciation to Spoof's musical genius. The greatness of Spoof Collins's work will never be forgotten. Collins, the Magic Music Man, has become immortal.

"Keeper of the Dream" (1954)

This bleak story features two main characters, Professor O'Hanion and Hunicutt. Both men are involved in scientific work, including the conquest of space through space travel and eventual colonization of the stars.

Scientists discover that Earth is the only thing that really exists, and everything outside of the Earth is an illusion. To reveal this shattering truth to humankind would be to destroy its dream for space travel and its dream that it is not alone in the universe. Knowing this, scientists decide not to reveal the truth to humankind in order to keep alive its dream of travel to other worlds to find other intelligences. Let humankind believe in an illusion.

Beaumont's point is tersely and directly stated: giving up faith is easier than giving up a dream. Faith is always secondary to the dream, and although it can assist in many ways, it can never replace the importance of that dream. The sociological theme of paradoxical perception is at work in all levels of the story, and in this instance, the shadow cast is more real than the figure which cast it. Illusion becomes the valid reality. A lie becomes the truth.

O'Hanion and Hunicutt become existential figures in a purposeless universe constructed upon a lie. Like many of Beaumont's stories, this one carries certain tenets of existential philosophy. Although romanticized to some extent, the thought remains: existence does take precedence over essence and humankind is responsible for its acts; the responsibility for these acts is a source of anguish for mankind, and to contain the terrifying loneliness of this anguish is to create a dream that gives meaning to existence and displaces meaninglessness or nothingness.

"Place of Meeting" (1954)

Big Jim Kroner and his group are tabulating the number of the dead on Earth following a man-made holocaust of gas bombs and disease in "Place of Meeting." The group consists of representatives from nationalities around the globe; these survivors are immortal, and they meet together near a deserted church. Even the wind blowing through the church and ringing its bell does not disturb them, for the bell tolls for dying humankind, not them. It is October, and they are the October People come together; and until civilization springs up anew from the destruction, these survivors must put away their dreams and retire to sleep. There is a tender scene in which Kroner interacts with the group and assures the young ones that better times will come again for them. The survivors change shapes, turning the air black and flapping away into the falling night. Directly, Kroner gets into his coffin, closes the lid, and falls asleep only to reawaken when humans come again—a time when the survivors can freely and quietly roam the Earth and feast on human blood. Until that time, they must sleep the long, lonely night.

An interesting approach to the traditional vampire story, "Place of Meeting" deals with reference group in a highly sophisticated manner. This group—the individuals by whose standards we judge ourselves—is vampiric in nature, and its role priorities are internalized accordingly. As a folk group or select minority, the vampire community eliminates structural prejudice towards it with the death of humankind. The definition of the situation, and what is considered normal and deviant, is controlled by the survivors.

Beaumont succeeds in creating what appears to be a normal situation in a seemingly ordinary gathering of people; then, the touch of fantasy comes into play. In the end

59

the vampires seem more genuinely humane and kind than the crass humans they have replaced.

"Mass for Mixed Voices" (1954)

This story focuses on what individuality comes to mean in a strictly regimentated, totalitarian society and how one man overcomes it, and by so doing, creates the role of poetic continuity in an otherwise conformity-ridden social structure. Johnmartin has entered Golden Time, and it is time for him to accept his societal role of death. He is summoned before his supervisor, but says that he does not want to die and prefers to go on living forever. A philosophical and religious conversation takes place between the two men, and Johnmartin maintains his request for immortality. This request is denied. He is taken away and allowed a brief stop at his garden; there, he greets his flowers and they reflect sadness at his leaving them. The flowers watch expectantly as the old man gathers their seeds and swallows them.

Johnmartin is put to death by the state, and his last wish to have his remains buried in his private garden are honored. Later, a single, unusual flower, having something precious in it from every other flower, blooms in the garden—the dream of immortality, the escape from the loneliness of death, is secured. Johnmartin will become one with the beauty and magic of the flowers. He welcomes the darkness marking the end of his earthly body with that sweet vision.

Social mask, role, death, pursuit of a dream, loneliness, and beauty are the major themes in this story. As in many of Beaumont's tales, the concept of social mask is evident: here Johnmartin's societal mask hides his true nature. Only through the shedding of the human form can the true essence of the poetic self become one with the universe of beauty and magic.

"Hair of the Dog" (1954)

This is the account of Lorenzo Gissing and his odd demise. Gissing is Everyman in search of immortality.

Gissing reacts to the death of a fellow university student named Bunky Frith by becoming absorbed in the study of death. He is visited by an insurance company representative who offers him a form of limited immortality in exchange for his soul; the contract is renewable every one hundred years. Payment, set on the first day of every month, is one plucked hair from Gissing's head, to be tendered on the day payment is due, but not one day before. Gissing agrees and looks forward to a dream of happiness, contentment, health, and unhampered existence. He marries Lady Anastasia Moseby and later becomes a playboy; not long afterwards, he starts losing his hair.

Down to one hair, he tries to relax by having a passionate night of sex with his wife. In the morning, the hair is gone, and after a frantic search, his wife discovers it in time for him to make the payment. Having gone to a hair specialist, Dr. Binkley, Gissing knows he will have sufficient hair in time for the next payment.

A representative from Asmodeus in Hades arrives and takes Gissing away, admonishing him for sending in a hair other than his own. The hair sent in for payment came from a brown-haired spaniel named Heine, a pet owned by Gissing's wife. Although Gissing's wife never sees her husband again, she continues to bear up well in the company of her faithful dog.

Behind the humor in this story is a commentary on roles, which is evident in one form or another throughout Beaumont's fiction. Role tolerance and role conflict share a narrow sidewalk, and when one individual disturbs another's role, beware of the consequences.

"The Jungle" (1954)

This story opens with a grief-stricken Richard Austin watching his wife Mag die; he cannot understand why she and his workers are dying and he alone has been spared. The unknown disease destroys the victim's blood cells as if they have been attacked by an angry virus, but the cause remains a mystery; destruction of body tissues leading to death is always the final stage. Alone, Austin ventures into the deserted city, Mbarara, the jungle city he created at the expense of all life there; he is the only white man in the area and Mbarara is his dream. A curse has been placed on the white men's works by a Bantu shaman named Bokawah; now, it is taking effect. Austin locates the native village and confronts Bokawah. The old shaman informs Austin that the reason he has been spared is so that he can carry the message back to white civilization that Mbarara must be abandoned or the disease will spread.

Austin defies the shaman's primitive magic and promises that thousands will come to the city and remove the superstitious natives from the area. Austin returns to his beloved city and becomes lost inside it; something has entered his mind causing confusion. Still, he fights on and refuses to give in; finally, he locates his residence and goes to his apartment and wife. Austin believes the magic of his civilization is stronger than the native magic, despite all that has happened to him and those around him. He opens the door and discovers his wife being eaten by a lion. Austin begins screaming in terror at the sight.

Death, pursuit of a dream, loneliness, role conflict, the primitive versus the civilized world, and nature versus the urban city are key themes in this story. Austin cannot accept that his way is inferior to the natives' life because he is a "civilized" man; he pays an appropriate price for his arrogance.

"The Murderers" (1955)

A study in deviance, "The Murderers" deals with violence in a sensate setting. This is the story of Herbert Foss and Ronald Raphael, two rich young men in pursuit of the ultimate thrill: murder.

The best of friends, Foss and Raphael decide to murder somebody, and set off in their quest to Bughouse Square in search for a suitable victim among the less fortunate; eventually, after watching different people from different walks of life pass by, they select an old man named James Oliver Fogarty. Fogarty is alone in the world, and he appears meek and humble enough to fit into their murder plans. They take Fogarty to their apartment and later identify themselves to him as social directors for the Y.M.C.A. They set out to get Fogarty drunk, and during the process, they become drunk as well. They awake to find Fogarty gone. They discover that he has robbed them of their possessions; their dream of the ultimate thrill is gone.

Despite their high social standing, their wealth and their cleverness, and their roles as elitists, both young men have been upstaged and outwitted by one of life's derelicts. Appearances are definitely not what they appear to be, and the sociological theme of paradoxical perception is evident during the story. Two bored, lonely young men, they end as they begin, impoverished personally if not financially.

The rich are different from others, Beaumont seems to be saying, especially the two young men of this engrossing story—they have everything that the material world has to offer, but they lack a sense of ethics and morality. To kill a human being for thrills merely reinforces the fact that both Foss and Raphael lack sensitivity to spirtual awareness and are incapable of any higher thoughts other than the pursuit of personal pleasure. Fogarty is a lively, interesting character, and his continued existence at the conclusion of the story indicates that the meek and humble do at times inherit the Earth.

"The Hunger" (1955)

One of Charles Beaumont's favorite creations, "The Hunger" is a poignant analysis of a lonely woman facing death. This is the story of Julia Landon, aged thirty-eight, and her life with her sisters; their existence is drab, controlled, and mechanical. Robert Oakes, an escaped murderer from an asylum, has eluded police and is on the prowl in Julia's area; he was sentenced to the asylum for raping and murdering his cousin, Patsy Blair. Like Julia, Oakes is a lonely person. Both Julia and Oakes are just faces in the crowd; each, in her or his own individual way, wears a mask of societal detachment to hide the fear, societal violence, and sexual needs lurking behind their masks. Their hunger to know somebody intimately in both the mental and physical sense, to reach out and touch another person's identity and dispel the loneliness of one's own personal identity, is overwhelming. The interaction and dialogue between the sisters is sensitive, revealing the role of each; role prioritization—the ranking in order of importance of the different roles an individual plays to minimize conflict—is sharply etched in each character.

Oakes is running from the police, and Julia is searching for his presence; their actions symbolize the need for human beings to communicate and reach out to each other in a sensate setting. The story concludes with the meeting of Julia and Oakes; essentially, both characters hope they will survive the encounter. The purifying, cleansing power of the rain touches this mismatched couple as they meet. Death is seen as a release from the horrors of earthly existence and as a bridge to a new beginning; whether death comes to either character is left to the imagination of the reader. In the final scene, the societal mask of each character is ripped away, revealing two lonely people confronting each other with the nakedness of his or her soul. The hunger in their souls will be satisfied. Essentially, they share the same dream.

"The Last Word" (1955)

Co-authored with Chad Oliver, this science fiction story is the first of several humorous pieces dealing with Claude Adams. Alone in the ruins of civilization, Adams returns in his self-designed time-machine to 2,000,000 B.C., where he encounters an android in the form of a woman; he oils her vital parts, and immediately she becomes more feminine and lively. She takes him to some telepathic Martians who have crash-landed on Earth while exploring the solar system; Adams repairs their spacecraft. In exchange for his services, the Martians leave him their female android which he names Eve. In time, they have a child—a male, greatly different from any human Adams has ever known—and he is named Son. Son is blessed with unusual powers.

Twelve years later, dissatisfied with his Eden, Adams leaves paradise via way of his time machine and arrives in 3042 A.D. He has now entered a time in Earth's future history where everything is controlled by The Big Machine; he is promptly arrested for curiosity. Adams manages to unplug the machine, and the result is the collapse of civilization into ruins. Now in the company of Eve and Son, he sets out to build a new civilization in 3042 A.D. The story concludes as Adams and Eve march into the bushes to begat a wife for Son.

This is a humorous, wry science fiction adventure, and in addition to telling the reader that history repeats itself, it also relates the idea that as long as curiosity exists, so will humankind—into whatever altered form it may develop. Despite the obvious philosophical and religious overtones, Beaumont's themes of death, loneliness, and pursuit of a dream take precedence, and are further strengthened by the anthropological themes of species curiosity and myth-making. It is also a humorous look at sexology.

"Free Dirt" (1955)

This is the story of a man named Mr. Aorta who believes in getting everything free from life that he can, whether it is by coupon, contest, or by devious means. Anything free must be taken advantage of completely. The story is a study in what the concept of *free* means, and for Mr. Aorta, getting things free is the essence of life. His lifestyle is dissected in detail, and at one point he travels to the Lilyvale Cemetery, which is offering free dirt; Aorta's plan is to grow seeds in it so that he might have a garden. As in many of Charles Beaumont's stories, the central character is a lonely individual, and Mr. Aorta is no exception: his life is centered around avoiding loneliness, which is why he pursues anything free. He considers his life to be a condensed version of Everyman with everything acted out symbolically. His garden is a success beyond his wildest dream. His dream has become reality to his perceptions. He harvests the garden and proceeds to eat, and eat, and eat. He has created, free, with his own hands and the free cemetery dirt, a miracle for eating. The free miracle must be devoured.

The story concludes when a neighbor, Joseph William Santucci, discovers Mr. Aorta's dead body; it is later found that Mr. Aorta ate himself to death, and the doctors find his stomach contains many pounds of dirt, and nothing else. Mr. Aorta is buried in the cemetery where the wind blows free.

Mr. Aorta is the existential man who gets everything free without working for it, including death. In essence, Mr. Aorta has pursued and secured three free things in life: destruction of a dream, loneliness, and death. Mr. Aorta dies an existential martyr to the pursuit of a miracle grown from nothingness which in turn returns to nothingness. This ranks as one of Beaumont's best philosophical stories.

"The New Sound" (1955)

One of Charles Beaumont's shortest fiction works, "The New Sound" is the story of Mr. Goodhew's dream to collect sounds. This bizarre fascination in his lonely existence consumes him until he has collected the sounds of the dying. Eventually, his collection expands to capture human death sounds; it becomes complete except for one: the sound of his own passing. He has the most complete collection in the world.

A nuclear war breaks out, and he rushes to record the sound of the dying, but when he starts to play it back, the recorder goes dead with all other power. He shakes the dead recorder as the world around him disintegrates. Overtaken by the destruction, he lets out a small cry of anguish, not for himself, but for missing the ultimate sound of nuclear death that he had sought to capture on tape. He is destroyed before he has time to scream out his own death cry.

The new sound is the sound of a sensate culture in its death throes, and the existential loneliness that will result when the world disintegrates into nothingness. Loneliness as a distinct component of social and personal role becomes apparent in a sensate setting where communication and sharing of affection have disappeared. People, afraid to interact and communicate with each other, take solace in their individualized private hells where none may enter and there is no exit. It is a bitter solace, at best.

In some ways, Charles Beaumont is an Americanized Albert Camus whose approach is related to individuality and the power of dreams. In many ways, too, Beaumont is as great a writer as Camus. Future Beaumont scholars will see the connection as more Beaumont work is published.

"The Vanishing American" (1955)

A very subtle story, this is the account of forty-seven-year-old man named Henry Minchell, who upon leaving his office discovers that he has lost his existence. It is his forty-seventh birthday, and on his way home he wonders why people stare through him as though he did not exist; stopping at a bar for a drink, he is ignored and leaves scared when he does not see his reflection in the mirror.

At home, his wife Madge and his son Jimmy fail to see his presence, and to his utter horror he discovers he is invisible. He can't be touched or touch, or even be heard. Images of his lost dreams float in his mind like so much dead driftwood. The fear of death haunts him, and he is afraid.

Drifting through the faceless city, he comes to the city library and there he mounts the back of a huge stone lion near the library steps. Tired, his spirit weary, he bemoans what he has become and cries. Suddenly, he finds people can see him again. Henry Minchell is alive again, and he has been given a second chance; this time, he will live life fully and fulfill his dreams, becoming an individual apart from the sameness of the crowd—the herd—which has been his lot until mounting the lion and submerging himself in a dream.

Although the paradoxical perception theme runs through the story from beginning to conclusion, and illusion and reality are blurred, a more important feature of this story is Beaumont's handling of role conflict in a technological society. The ability to dream has been lost to Minchell, and without dreams, he is dead and has vanished piece by piece, until one day he is gone and existence is denied him. By regaining his dreams of what he is capable of achieving, he escapes the crowd and becomes alive once again, an individual in a country of vanishing Americans.

The Crooked Man" (1955)

A vivid image study in sexual deviance and ethics, this story illustrates two of Beaumont's major themes: the sanctity of personal dreams and aspirations, and individuality. Decades after its publication, it remains a controversial science fiction work. Set far in the future, the United States has now become a nation of homosexuals, and artificial insemination has been practiced for several centuries to eliminate the perverted act of sexual intercourse between a man and a woman. Homosexuality is the law of the land; heterosexuality is illegal and immoral. Anyone going against the societal dictates concerning sexuality is labeled crooked and mentally ill. *The Finger Dance*—running the fingers over the solar plexus while tapping the digits in a sinuous hopping dance—along with *The Tongue Dance* are two accepted social symbols for homosexual contact. A lonely young man named Jesse is attempting to convince a lonely young woman named Mina that a relationship and sexual activity between a man and a woman is normal, and that homosexuality is abnormal. Jesse and Mina are not allowed to fulfill their relationship as a couple, for the story concludes as Jesse is arrested and taken away for the cure. Afterwards, Jesse will be returned to society as a normal homosexual male, and the vice squad policeman assures him of this fact in lewd terms. Jesse, the crooked man, will be made societally straight, and Mina will be treated to eliminate any confusion she may have contracted from Jesse during the short time they were together.

Society is the murderer of the right to have personal dreams in this complex and tragic morality tale involving role conflict, symbol systems, stratification, and labeling. The right to be different has been replaced with conformity to sensate directives.

"Last Rites" (1955)

One of Beaumont's more philosophical stories, "Last Rites" concerns a Catholic priest's encounter with an android. Father Courtney is the parish priest to a small parish in the country; he goes to meet George Donovan, who is dying. Father Courtney and George Donovan have known each other for twenty years. To the priest's dismay, his friend confesses that he is not a human being at all, but an artificial man—an android—over a century old and worried about his soul. The priest and Donovan engage in a deeply philosophical and religious conversation concerning death and the afterlife, and Donovan requests that the priest give him Extreme Unction, even though he is a machine. To give Extreme Unction, or last rites, to a machine goes against everything the priest has ever known throughout his life or been taught through church doctrine.

The priest finally accepts the truth that Donovan is not human and does administer the last rites to his friend; much later, he will disassemble Donovan and tell the parishioners that this gentle but firm old man with the soft voice and patient manner has moved away to an unspecified place. The story concludes with the priest blinking away tears, asking forgiveness for the act he has to perform out of friendship. As an android, Donovan comes across as more sensitive and more human than most of the men in this story; his kindness is self-evident.

What makes this remarkable story different from many others employing the same theme is Beaumont's treatment of the role of the soul in a technological setting, and its implications for a society placing emphasis on the sensate approach to existence rather than the ideational. "Last Rites" is reminiscent of certain thoughts expressed in Thomas à Kempis's (1380-1471) meditative work, *The Imitation of Christ*.

"A Point of Honor" (1955)

Originally published as "I'll Do Anything," "A Point of Honor" is a tightly-knit excursion into ethnicity. It concerns the coming of age of Julio Velasquez and the effect of peer pressure on a Mexican-American youth.

Velasquez seeks to join a gang called the *Aces*, and is brought to the attention of this group by his friend, Danny Arriaga. Throughout the plot the reader is given an excellent portrait of minority lifestyle; the themes of initiation and rite of passage are clearly developed, along with societal role. The dialogue in this story, as in other Beaumont fictions, is sharp and clear, and reveals the speaker's role and personality attributes in a subtle fashion. Julio reflects the influence of significant others—people who have special impact or effect on an individual's personality—throughout the story, and although he has a sensitive nature that the others lack in this sensate atmosphere, he nonetheless accepts the knife given to him by the group leader, Paco. The knife, used as a sociological symbol in this story, will perform its function in three ways: to act as a weapon of destruction in a sensate society, to sever the existence of the perceived enemy's reality, and to establish the reality of the knife's owner as superior.

Julio meditates on death and on the fact that he must use the knife to kill a movie theater assistant manager; to murder the individual is the initiation required for Julio to join the *Aces*. The reason this man must be killed is because he insulted the *Aces* and downgraded them as an ethnic group.

Julio does not want to kill the manager, but peer pressure coupled with his societal role as a minority figure in America forces him to become angry; as the anger builds, and he considers his Mexican heritage, he makes the decision to commit the murder. In a land of shadows, Julio must eliminate a shadow to establish his identity as the valid one. The story concludes as Julio approaches the faceless shadow of the assistant manager with his knife.

"A Classic Affair" (1955)

Dave Jenkinson is being informed by his former love, Ruth Osterman, that she is leaving her husband Hank after one year of marriage because he is unfaithful to her. Dave would like to replace the Osterman weekends with the Jenkinson weekends, and regain his lost love; he agrees to help Ruth in the hope that he can rid himself of Hank. Dave follows Hank and confronts him with Ruth's tale of suspected infidelity. Hank, in a most peculiar way, agrees, then takes Dave to meet the other woman. The other woman turns out to be a 1929 Duesenberg automobile at *Springfield's Vintage Automobiles* car lot.

Dave, realizing all is not well with his friend, agrees to sit inside the car while Hank tells him about the situation. To Dave's surprise, Hank confesses that he is in love with the Duesenberg; when he is away from the car, his life is miserable—the car is Hank's woman, his love, his happiness. Seeking to get Ruth for himself, Dave purchases the car; he plans to exchange the Duesenberg for Ruth and knows Hank will go along in his obsession with the car. But the more Dave drives the luxury car, the longer he puts off his plan for exchange. Towards the conclusion of the story, the reader knows that Dave will become a slave to the car as Hank was, and Ruth will be forgotten. The 1929 Duesenberg is a complex machine, and in a technological society, complexity is oftentimes more exciting and stimulating than a simple unclassic love affair between a man and a woman. In this strange love triangle, the Duesenberg is the center of attraction between Hank and Dave.

The Duesenberg serves as both cause and effect in the relationship, and offers both men a sense of compensation that allows only for a pleasure and servitude which both men can enjoy without fear of demands by another human being; unconsciously, rather than take a chance on human relationships, both men opt far the safety of a mechanical relationship with the Duesenberg.

"Traumerei" (1956)

This story concerns a young man who is scheduled to be executed for murder. He believes that when he dies he will awake from the execution, and the world he has been a part of will vanish. Then, he will confront a new punishment, and the process will repeat itself. He dreams what is happening to him, and everything exists in his imagination. Each time he is killed, he will awaken again into a new and different world.

The theme is simply stated throughout the plot, and the characters interact and react as masked harlequins in a morality play that has no ending, only a series of existential repetitions. What is significant about this story is that it illustrates a key theme moving throughout Beaumont's career as a mainstream fiction writer: dream replaces faith in importance; pursuit of a dream gives meaning to an otherwise meaningless existence. When one loses the ability to pursue a dream or partake in the substance of a dream, no matter what type of dream it may be, then ones loses the reason for existence and struggle.

Death and loneliness are evident in "Traumerei," but the overriding symbol and theme is dream. Charles Beaumont was fascinated with dream symbology, and there are Jungian overtones to his reliance on this symbol. Dream as a symbol is found in the literature of all nations, from the past to the present; interpretation of its social and individual importance varies from one culture to another. Dream can be both reality and illusion or one or the other, depending upon its application to the social reality in which it exists at a given time. For Beaumont, dream is connected to the psyche; to pursue any dream is to pursue the quest for an individualized Holy Grail of Essence and Truth.

"I, Claude" (1956)

Co-authored with Chad Oliver, this science fiction story is a further adventure of the Claude Adams who first appeared in "The Last Word." Whatever clichés were left untouched in the first story are now satirized in this pastiche. This tale casts Adams in a god-like capacity as a ruler and warlord. He encounters several writers and their creations, including Merlin, Donald Duck, Tarzan, Grendel, Count Dracula, and Robin Hood, among others. Adams also finds aliens and the eternal female, this time in the form of Woola, the beautiful Princess of Sarboom (in a pastiche of Edgar Rice Burroughs's Mars series). Earth is eventually destroyed, and once again Adams finds himself cast as the father of the future. The story ends as a much older Adams and his Woola wander eastward into the sunrise—the new Adam and the new Eve, so to speak.

"I, Claude" has humor, high adventure, philosophical musings, and all of the complexity required to create a successful satire. In addition to the religious, philosophical, and historical overtones, we also find the themes of death, loneliness, and pursuit of a dream.

The function of role is also examined in this amusing companion piece to "The Last Word." As comic science fiction, both "I, Claude" and "The Last Word" can stand separately or together as a fine example of this type of humorous fantasy. By matching the comic abilities of Beaumont and Oliver together, two highly original stories have resulted. Both stories are funny and entertaining reading, and should not be missed by fans of either writer.

"The Monster Show" (1956)

Written at a time when television was in its infancy, Beaumont gives the reader a scathing look at what the future holds for the viewer. This futuristic tale concentrates on one television network's attempt to successfully capture the viewing attention of the world for the showing of its special, "The Monster Show." The show has been hyped and promoted well in advance of its airdate, and all humankind has tuned in with great anticipation. The show is literally saturated with product advertising. At the conclusion of the showing, the man in the executive suite responsible for the program is greeted by slimy, unproboscidean-faced, lavender creatures; being one of them, he quickly rejects his human disguise and assumes his true form. His true name is Volshak, and he basks in his fellow creatures' approval and compliments. They ask Volshak how he achieved the effect of putting humankind to sleep, making it possible for them to eliminate all human beings. Volshak thinks of the advertising and commercials, and replies that it was easy. With humankind dead at its television sets, lulled to sleep by the boredom of commercial advertising, the aliens can now proceed without fear to colonize Earth with their own people.

Beaumont here makes a satirical comment on the future of television—a media dominated by slick commercials injected into the bloodstream of regular programming at a steady and deadening pace. "The Monster Show" guarantees the Earth will not go out with a bang or a whimper, but with a mere snore of indifference. A humorous look at primary deviance, this story also examines norms and symbol systems in a sensate cultural setting. Television is the invited guest in the home and serves as a medium for interaction processes; the medium is the message.

"You Can't Have Them All" (1956)

Doctor Lenardi is examining Edward Simms, who is twenty-eight years old; tired and physically worn out: his appearance suggests that that he is someone around forty-eight years old. Something has caused Simms to age prematurely and has affected his mind in the process. Simms begins his tale by comparing himself at first to Dante with an attachment for beautiful women; each time he encounters one, he must make love to her. Over a period of time, this fascination affects his mind, and despite his continuous exhaustion, he continues to track down his special type of woman. He is trying to reach each one and complete his task before a new crop appears on the scene and reaches age eighteen. To miss his deadline will cause him to perish from exhaustion. Simms begs the doctor for a stimulant so that he may complete his task. Instead, Dr. Lenardi gives the young-old man some medication that will knock him out of commission for a couple of weeks. During that time, a new crop of women will reach their eighteenth birthday, and Simms will have to start again. The doctor tells Simms he can't have them all, and reveals to Simms that one of Simms's type happens to be the doctor's wife, Alice. The look on Simms's face becomes a definition of terror.

In an ironic, almost prophetic fashion, the fate that befell Simms also hit Beaumont some eleven years later, when the author died from premature Alzheimer's disease on February 21, 1967. But it was not the pursuit of women that killed Beaumont, only the degeneration of his brain. And Beaumont, like Simms, slipped into a twilight world and perish utterly alone. Also featured in this story are the themes of sexual mores, role, definition of the situation, and how humans define a meaningful existence and lifestyle.

"Last Night the Rain" (1956)

Originally published as "Sin Tower," "Last Night the Rain" involves the theme of the outsider coupled with the idea that the individual must act if he or she is to give meaning to personal existence, no matter what the consequences of that act. It is the story of Amy, Josh, and Beckman, a story of unrealized sexual union on the physical plane of existence, in which the couple find sanctity and spiritual union only in death.

Amy is a pretty, innocent fourteen-year-old with soft big eyes. Josh, who is about the same age as Amy, is attracted to her but afraid of the awakening of his manhood and sexuality. Beckman, the old man who lives in the houseboat by the river, is as strange in his peculiar way as Amy and Josh are; he has built two towers made of stacked rocks in the sand, and he claims God commanded him to build them. He calls the large one the Sin Tower, and the smaller, unfinished one the Tower of Good. Amy wants to run away with Beckman, but he rejects her; she runs to the Sin Tower which collapses on her when she attempts to scale it. She is killed, and Josh runs away. Beckman gently carries Amy into the river like a sacrificial victim; both disappear into the stream and are never found.

Later, the community dismisses the incident as two crazies getting together. The river becomes both metaphor and biblical symbol in this story. It is visualized as representing woman with all of her complexity and sexual drives, and as a biblical cleansing agent in a sensate cultural setting. The towers serve as both phallic symbols and as guideposts to an impartial God. The beckoning message Amy hears in the rain is her womanhood calling to be fulfilled. In death, the river brings fourteen-year-old Amy together with Beckman: Innocence and Wisdom are finally united. Like "Black Country," this story is one of Beaumont's finest mainstream fiction works.

"The Dark Music" (1956)

Like many of Beaumont's short fiction works, "The Dark Music" deals with the sociophilosophical theme of the outsider—the individual who is at odds with the rest of the community or environment for varying reasons. As a major theme in Beaumont's work, it can be found to some degree in all of his writing. This story concerns Miss Lydia Maple of Sand Hill; she is an unmarried biology teacher on a field trip with her students.

Miss Maple is a woman afraid of sex, and she considers herself pure and above the animal pleasures of sexuality. The story opens on a pastoral, idyllic setting. Maple awakens from a gentle slumber to the sound of flutes in the forest; she is enchanted by the music and attempts to follow it. Her reverie is shattered by a young student named William who finds her, and she returns to her ordered, normal, pristine existence. Later, she falls under the spell of the forest and its music; her visits there become like melodic, sweet dreams. As if awakening from a separate, sensual reality, she discovers herself naked in the grove of the forest.

Realization comes to her that she has been a lover to the great Greek God, Pan; pregnant, and craving the sweet lust of what she had once known in the forest, she flees the memories of Sand Hill and the grove and moves away forever. Nobody knows why she left; nobody cares.

A story of illusion and reality, "The Dark Music" is a tale about a woman's rite of passage. Miss Lydia Maple moves from the stage of puritanism and fettered female societal role to the stage of sensual woman, and finally to that of liberated woman unafraid of her role as passionate, thinking woman in a man's world.

A well-crafted story with Jungian overtones, this story suggests the sociological themes of paradoxical perception, identity search, and role conflict. Societal encumbrances give way to nature's sanctity and role priorities are established.

"The Face of a Killer" (1956)

Frank Lampredi is having Dr. Donohue perform plastic surgery on his face so that he looks like Gianinni Musso. After a life of criminal activities, he wants to give up this lifestyle; his dream is to become a decent, respected citizen of the community and no longer suffer the loneliness of being on the run from the authorities. Gianinni Musso is a banker and is what Lampredi desires to become. He has studied Musso in detail and knows how to mask himself accordingly. The plastic surgery takes place, and Lampredi becomes Musso. He assumes Musso's role.

Everything goes as planned, and Lampredi sneaks into the banker's bedroom and slays the sleeping victim

78

with a knife; he hides the body in a car and plans to dispose of it later. The body, wrapped up and hidden like a mummy in the trunk of his car, assures Lampredi he is in control of his dream and on his way to respectability as Musso.

He walks into Musso's bank and greets everybody as Musso would do, but his appearance terrifies the bank employees. He is informed that the real Musso died of a heart attack a week ago and that the estate was left to Musso's housekeeper, Mrs. St. Claire. He thinks of the dead body in his car and realizes he has killed the house-keeper who was sleeping in the master bedroom. Lampredi is arrested and laughs at the irony of the situation; much later, when he is strapped into the electric chair to die for murder, he is still laughing.

Dream, loneliness, death, and social masking make this fast-paced mystery story into a murder morality tale with its subtle structure; going back for further readings, the scholar and reader will discover themes in this story that will occupy Beaumont throughout his writing career.

"Father, Dear Father" (1957)

Originally published as "Oh, Father of Mine." A fifty-three-year-old man, Mr. Pollet, is obsessed with the dream of going back in time to kill his father. Pollet con-structs a time machine after numerous failed attempts; it returns him and his .38 revolver to Middleton, Ohio on February 19, 1916. He confronts his father, murders him, escapes, and returns to the present. Nothing happens to Pollet and he does not vanish. He has killed the cruel man and yet he still exists. Pollet destroys his time machine and tells his wife of what he has accomplished; and, during the course of the conversation, she tells him that the photo-graph of his father does not resemble him and that he killed the wrong man despite going to the right time coordinates.

Mr. Pollet realizes his error and is horrified at the simple truth of the situation: literally, he is the son of a bitch. The man he had always believed to be his father was not his father at all.

A deadly, on-target comment on adultery, this story also reflects Beaumont's concern with the role of a child in societal situation where love is denied a child in one form or another. An aspect of Beaumont that is part of his fictional world is his love for children and their role in a stable family environment; that the pressures of an urban world distort the role of a child as contrasted with a rural setting can be seen in this story of the lonely Mr. Pollet. As civilization becomes more urbanized and technological, children become as things to possess and use rather than as small human beings requiring love and nurturement.

A story of role conflict, "Father, Dear Father" also features the sociological themes of self-fulfilling prophecy and depersonalization. Paradoxical perception affects Mr. Pollet's definition of the situation throughout the plot.

"Fair Lady" (1957)

This is the account of a school teacher named Miss Elouise; she is growing old and is afraid of dying without having loved. A lonely woman, she is searching for a tall stranger to love her. She meets a bus driver, Oliver O'Shaugnessy, and immediately falls in love with him; each morning, she rides the bus to where she teaches and has a silent, unspoken love affair with O'Shaugnessy. This situation lasts for three years until the driver is transferred to the Randolphe route.

Miss Elouise realizes she must make a decision concerning the remainder of her life, and she retires from teaching. She moves to a new location and a new bus corner, and patiently waits to ride the bus route with Oliver O'Shaugnessy.

This is the tender story of a woman approaching old age without ever having loved and communicated that love. Elouise, afraid of disappointment, will live out her fantasy as a face in the crowd riding a bus to nowhere, content with the fantasy world she has created around O'Shaugnessy. Her fantasy—her dream—becomes her reality in illusion.

Beaumont shows that loneliness can be tempered by dreams, even if a particular dream is unrealized; it is the simple act of possessing the dream that gives vitality and life to the individual having it. An unrealized dream is better than nothing as one approaches death, and it is better perhaps to have dreamed a great love—whatever that love may be—than to have gone through life with no dream (or love) at all.

The concept of love is examined in this story, as is the concept of role from the perspectives of social and individual analyses of role. Aware of her societal role, it is only near the end of her life that Elouise is brave enough to face the consequences of being an individual in a technological society that demands role conformity, if only through a fantasy.

"Nursery Rhyme" (1957)

This is the tension-filled account of Agnes and Randolph Phillips and their son, Carlie Lee Phillips; a bizarre look at the nuclear family, it points out that Americans are more attached to their children while they are young and less attached to their children as adults. The story concerns Carlie Lee Phillips seeking shelter with his parents; having gotten drunk, he had attempted to have sexual intercourse with the Withers girl and during the struggle he hits her and runs. Carlie is being pursued by the authorities, and they have tracked him to his parents' home. Carlie Lee flees to his old room in the house, and there reflects on the room and its contents; his childhood memories surface, and he fires and empties his revolver into objects in the room. The mother enters the room, ignores Carlie, and goes directly to the empty bed where an imaginary baby Carlie is and talks to the baby; within minutes, the authorities enter and take Carlie away.

Agnes refuses to believe anything but a baby Carlie exists; for her, it is better to have the dream of a baby son than an adult son who will one day disappear. The imaginary baby has simple demands that Agnes can cope with, but a real adult son has parental demands she cannot and does not want to handle. Agnes hated Carlie for growing up and becoming a man and leaving her. Randolph walks the thin line of reality, inhabiting both Agnes's dream illusion and the reality of his son's presence in the house after the rape attempt.

A study in role and definition of the situation, "Nursery Rhyme" also centers on the pursuit of dream, loneliness, and dying. Modern society has extracted its toll on the family from each member of the Phillips household; each suffers from a scarred psyche.

"Tears of the Madonna" (1957)

Charles Beaumont had the technical skill and creative ability to invest much of his mainstream fiction with a subtle, ofttimes poetic, touch of fantasy; this story reveals that skill and ability to its fullest.

"Tears of the Madonna" concerns human spirit and the social symbols that work against it to seek its destruction. It is the story of Ramón de Castro, who has arrived to see his first bullfight. A young man, it becomes apparent that he has never known a woman, and with the help of a pimp, he arranges for a sexual liaison with a woman of the streets named Delores. But surface appearances are deceiving, and Delores is more than she appears; before his contact with her, Ramón watches her perform on stage at the *Teatro de la Alegoria* in an allegorical performance. To his shock, Ramon realizes Delores has the true face of the Madonna, seen so often in paintings and art work; religious imagery comes into play, and sexuality blends with mysticism and religion. Later, before rites of passage and sexual intercourse can take place, Ramón runs away in fear and terror as he confronts the Madonna who gives her love unselfishly to all, and who is there to initiate him into the role of sexuality.

82

To the Beaumont scholar and reader, this story will be met with enthusiasm, for it is one of his most complex stories. It carries subtle themes that weave together in perfect harmony, such as religious imagery and the Grail quest, sexuality and sensuality, Fall from Grace, Salvation and Redemption, pursuit of dream, loneliness, death, social symbols, role, and social masks.

"Tears of the Madonna" is one of Beaumont's most perfect fictional creations. It exhibits every skill and theme Beaumont possessed as a writer. Ramón is the child-adult caught between two worlds, and remains one of Beaumont's most memorable and sensitive character creations.

"The Love-Master" (1957)

The story opens as the old love-master, Salvadori, is explaining to Mr. Cubbison that Cubbison's wife Beatrice is not frigid and requires only the proper key to unlock her sensuality. Salvadori advises The Chinese Flip method of lovemaking; the next evening Cubbison returns to say the method failed. Salvadori then suggests The Australian Hop method; it, too, fails, and Salvadori becomes frustrated, suggesting a method called The Drunken Reptile. Several other lovemaking techniques are tried to no avail, forcing Salvadori to make his first housecall in fifteen years to personally accept the challenge of sexually stimulating and satisfying the young woman.

Salvadori carries through his plan with complete success, then quickly exits so the young husband can enter the bedroom and continue on. The following evening, Cubbison returns, thanks Salvadori, and pays the old love-master for his services. But Cubbison refuses to leave, and strips naked. Salvadori is shocked, realizing that the beautiful woman before him is in reality Beatrice, and that the husband was an illusion which never existed. The story concludes as Beatrice sexually assaults the bewildered Salvadori for a night of intense sexual pleasure.

The subtle idea of social masking and the role of woman as the ultimate liberated human being rather than man is seen in this humorous encounter; the sociological theme of paradoxical perception is evident, as is the theme of accomodation for personal equilibrium. Male symbol systems are displaced by feminism, and the old love-master is entrapped by his own set of prescriptions—certain things an individual must do according to the opinion of society. What starts as role conflict for Beatrice becomes role tolerance, while the reverse holds true for Salvadori. The final confrontation between both characters involves a rite of passage where each will move on to a new stage of growth or social acceptance.

"In His Image" (1957)

Written originally as a short story (under the title "The Man Who Made Himself") this tale was later adapted as a teleplay by Beaumont for *The Twilight Zone*, having been televised on January 3, 1963. "In His Image" remains one of the finest segments to be shown on that series, and it is ranked as one of actor George Grizzard's finest acting performances. In the television version, actor Grizzard played the roles of both Alan Talbot and Walter Ryder, Jr. This is the story of an android created in his maker's image. Alan Talbot is a duplicate of Walter Ryder, Jr. Although flawed, Talbot represents everything that Ryder dreams of becoming but fears he cannot. Talbot is revealed as personable, and Ryder is revealed as lonely and bitter at his lot in life. Ryder has achieved his dream of creating a perfect duplicate, and despite its flaws, he realizes it has more potential within its structure than he has as a lonely human being. He has created the dream, and he must chose whether to live it or abandon it; he discovers that Talbot has fallen in love with a lovely young woman named Jessica. A death struggle ensues between the android and the man, and both fight for the right to fulfill the dream, escape loneliness, and escape immediate death. Ryder wins and Talbot is destroyed. The story concludes as a fearful yet hopeful Ryder attempts to pick up where the android left off and meets Jessica.

84

Ryder accepts the role definition the android has given him, and by doing this, he begins to live the dream fully he had never thought he could; death will eventually come to Ryder as it does to all humans, but the point is to live life fully until that moment arrives, and to overcome the existential loneliness we all face daily.

"The Infernal Bouillabaisse" (1957)

This is the account of Edmund Peskin and his dream to create a recipe that will assure him of immortality among his peers in the Gourmet's Club. He creates the masterpiece known as Bouillabaisse à la Peskin, which no other gourmet can ever surpass. The jealousy and hatred that arises over his refusal to divulge its contents finally causes Mr. Frenchaboy to fetch it; when he cannot get it through the normal channels, he simply murders Peskin to possess the secret. It is Mr. Frenchaboy's dream to surpass Peskin, and so he destroys the recipe.

Frenchaboy is arrested for murder, and his last request is that he be served the bouillabaisse à la Peskin. Since the recipe is unknown and has been destroyed, Frenchaboy's sentence to hang is delayed. Frenchaboy is clever, but not quite clever enough. He eats nothing but malted milks and hamburgers, and ultimately dies of acute indigestion.

Beaumont is having fun with this story, but in his manner as an astute satirist, he is also being deadly serious by making the point that those things we desire the most in life may become the very things that kill us or bring us loneliness. Another point seen in this very short story is that stratified approaches to living tend to produce static lifestyles and roles lacking in creativity. Although some dreams are deadly and can result in dire consequences, the main thrust must be to pursue a dream, for a person without a dream is a shattered and empty individual. To seek out a dream is to have some reason for existence in a purposeless universe. In the case of both Peskin and Mr.

Frenchaboy, they each achieve their dream, even though in the final analysis, it leads to each of their deaths.

"Open House" (1957)

Eddie Pierce, a lonely man and a nondescript face in the crowd, has murdered his wife Emma on All Fools' Day because she has killed his dreams with her insensitive ways during their short two years of marriage. He is suddenly surprised by the unexpected visit of Lew Hoover and Vernon F. Fein. Hoover relates to Fein Pierce's life story, revealing that Pierce was a fine writer who wanted to write novels but instead married Emma and became a butcher in a meat market. Unfortunately, Pierce also has to murder Hoover and Fein in the bathroom where he has his dead wife stored to keep her murder a secret. Pierce is making preparations to butcher the bodies when Len Brooks arrives: another guest, another murder. It is open house for Eddie Pierce on All Fools' Day, and Pierce realizes that the killing must continue to cover up the original murder.

This is the story of a bitter man driven to rage because his dreams have been destroyed. If he can't regain his dreams without such an act, then he is doomed to live out his life in an existential void; by exercising his will, he brings existence into a static situation, and even if he achieves chaos out of nothingness, he at least succeeds in displacing that deadly nothingness. Having suffered a role loss—when the role is reduced in importance so that the individual suffers a blow to his sense of self—and unable to live with it, Pierce can only redeem his sense of self and worth by open rebellion.

Pierce's rebellion is taken out on Emma, not because she is a woman, but because she represents the standardized wants and needs of a sensate society where the ends justify the means. But Pierce will never be able to eliminate all the societal attributes that threaten him, his sense of self, or his dreams, because there are too many of them confronting him.

86

RUNNING FROM THE HUNTER

"Night Ride" (1957)

This excellent companion piece to Beaumont's "Black Country" ranks as one of the author's finest mainstream short fictions; it illustrates Beaumont's mastery of characterization, dialogue, setting, and metaphor. Narrated by trumpeter Deacon Jones, this is the account of a lonely young jazz pianist named David Green. Green is a young widower when he joins the Band of Angels; due largely to his piano performances, including their trademark song, "Night Ride," and "Deep Shores," the group becomes quite successful and is able to cut many new records. Green falls in love with a beauty named Lorraine Schmidt who becomes a steady fixture in his life; the loneliness and sadness he has known begins to fade away. The band manager and bass player, Max Dailey, fearing that the young couple will marry and Green leave the band, deliberately lies to the musician, and tells him that Max has had sexual relations with Lorraine. Green's hope of finding a new life of happiness with another woman whom he can love as deeply as his dead wife is destroyed. He commits suicide with a razor. Later, Dailey says they are not a jazz band but a traveling morgue of dead dreams; he has only succeeded in collecting together a group of musicians who need to have their dreams destroyed to get the true blues sound. Dailey is ultimately deserted by his band and left alone; his own dream of achieving the real sound of jazz is also destroyed. Deacon Jones leaves Daily with an old .38 revolver and walks out of the room, knowing that there is no place for him to go either.

Beaumont's "Night Ride" and "Black Country" share the emotional intensity found in the short novel, *The Fall*, written by Albert Camus (1913-1960). A comparison can be made between the three works showing the emphasis in each on the individual's inescapable solidarity with his fellow human beings. Role, death, loneliness, pursuit of a dream, and social mask are the central themes in "Night Ride."

"Laugh Till You Die" (1957)

Co-authored with well-known writer William F. Nolan, this mystery story originally appeared under the joint byline of Frank Anmar. Jessica Randall, Alan Cole, and Paul Bowers make up the deadly love triangle in this fast-paced thriller set in a funhouse near Santa Monica, California.

Appearances are deceiving in this story, and the sociological theme of paradoxical perception leads the reader into the labyrinth of a clever killer's mind—who is the real murderer and who did the actual killing? Carefully structured, the story provides the reader with several possible interpretations of the ending. Cole is searching for Bowers and discovers him in the funhouse, where he has been told to go; there, he finds the strangled, lifeless body of Jessica hanging naked from a ceiling beam. Bowers has murdered Jessica because she was in love with Cole, and now seeks Cole's death also. Cole confronts Bowers. A chase and struggle ensue, and Bowers is killed with his own hunting knife; later, Cole tells to the police what has happened. But the matter is not ended, for a letter is sent to the police incriminating Cole; written by Bowers, it tells the cops what Cole is capable of. Entrapped by the letter, Cole is caught up in the Hollywood world of illusion and shadow, and becomes the victim of his own victimizing. The story concludes with Cole being confronted by the police: he starts laughing like the mechanical man at the funhouse. Cole has been snared by the illusion of his own perverted dreams, just as Bowers and Jessica were.

A fast-paced mystery story, "Laugh Till You Die" examines the symbols of love and power in Hollywood, and the affects of a sensate California lifestyle upon social and personal role. Death, role conflict, and violence are all key themes in this mystery story.

"Mainwaring's Fair Dinkum" (1957)

This outrageously humorous story reveals Charles Beaumont as a satirist at his best; from the beginning to the end of this adventure, Beaumont sets out to parody jungle adventure articles, and achieves the effect with stunning effectiveness. The story open on a half-asleep Mainwaring suddenly beset by a beautiful jungle woman called Takeena; aroused, he wants to have sex with her as she begins the subtle steps of the *kadota*, the Wagayan rite of fertility. But before he can realize his sexual goals, his American friend Rocky Crag interrupts him; he dispatches Crag on a quest and then sexually satisfies Takeena. The following day, Mainwaring and Crag start on their search; on the way they are attacked by jungle savages and taken captive, later being sentenced to the Death of the Two Virgins. They are taken to the Valley of Umba-Goona with two virgin women, set free, and left to whims of a monster.

Mainwaring learns of the monster's needs, and he and Crag quickly engage in sexual intercourse with the maidens and deflower the young women of their innocence. The monster appears, realizes what has happened, and disgustedly lumbers off into the jungle. Abandoning the women, the two men spend two lost weeks wandering in the jungle; hungry, they draw straws, and Mainwaring kills and eats Crag for food. Several near-death adventures befall the hero, Mainwaring, but he is never alone: there is always something to occupy his attention, and throughout his tribulations, he maintains his dream of securing the rock-tailed grebe. He gains his prize and finally reaches civilization. Directly, the Foundation will send him out on a new adventure in Central America in search of an even rarer creature called the Blue-Hackled Haggis.

Throughout this story, Beaumont presents the themes of death, fear of being alone, and pursuit of a dream. Mainwaring may have abandoned faith, but never once does he abandon his dream of possessing the rock-tailed grebe. The concept of social role interwoven with personal role is always evident.

"The Customers" (1957)

"The Customers" is an insightful look at the role of the elderly in the United States. Myrtle and Henry Ludlow are two elderly people waiting for death to call upon them; married and together, each wonders who will be called first. Death comes to call in the form of a young man dressed in black carrying a briefcase. He makes arrangements for the couple's interment at Murmuring Everglades Cemetery; the arrangements are made to the couple's demands and satisfaction.

Later, relieved that their personal arrangements have been completed, the couple retire to bed and fall asleep. The story concludes with the only sound coming from their bed being the sound of their brown cat purring.

All things lead to, and conclude in, death and dissolution. This is the point of the story: to live life fully until that final moment arrives. Death comes to everybody—it will never lack for a steady flow of customers—and that simple fact must never be forgotten. The Ludlows have each other, but they are also lonely; they are elderly, and in the United States the young do not have time for the elderly. Myrtle and Henry Ludlow have a dream of going on together for a short time longer, and they never know for sure when Death will arrive unexpectedly.

The idea that it is better to have a small dream than no dream at all is evident in this poignant story of the elderly. The couple's societal and personal role as an elderly married couple reflects how they are forced aside by a sensate society where the emphasis is on youth.

"A Death in the Country" (1957)

Originally published as "The Deadly Will to Win." Buck Larsen, tired and exhausted, is trying to reach the town of Grange, where he will soon be racing; he is a car driver who has grown old and is past his prime to handle the big money races. As he drives through the rain, he realizes that his friends in the racing Business are either dead, retired, or in business for themselves; he is now alone. He drives a Chevy, and like Larsen, the Chevy is battle-scarred survivor of the race track; neither will quit until death calls them off the race track.

Later, at the Soltan track during the qualifying runs, Larsen encounters a young man named Tommy Linden and Linden's girlfriend. Linden is driving to win and to impress his girl. The race ends with Larsen winning $350 and Linden dying in a car wreck. Larsen takes his winnings and drives off towards the next race and the next encounter with death. He thinks briefly of the young dead man, and reminds himself to work on his Chevy engine; then again, as the story ends, maybe he won't work on the engine at all. Role tolerance has given way to role loss.

Larsen is a veteran—a survivor in life—but he has grown weary. He realizes he can't keep up the pace indefinitely. Given the idea that those the gods favor die young, Larsen has been cheated of that glory and reduced to eking out small earnings through minor races; once at the peak of his profession, he is now watching himself fade out and vanish. He is a displaced, vanquished Apollo in a sensate society that has no use for yesterday's heroes, and Larsen must finish out his existence aware of that bitter fact; he will never die at zenith of his profession and be remembered, but at low tide: the memory of his deeds will be forgotten and washed away. In Larsen's emphasis on the sensate lifestyle, he must suffer and pay the price for his youthful advances against his life account until it is settled in full. Death will soon claim Larsen at the Last One Dollar Bet Window, and Larsen knows it.

"The Train" (1957)

Autobiographical in tone, "The Train" concerns a young boy's loss of innocence. While his mother is sleeps in the berth of the train, Neely slips out to explore the mystery and magic of the train; he believes that the train is his world, and as he passes through different sections, the images of the outside world with all of its ugliness fades, as does the images of his mother and father.

Every part of the train takes on a sense of wonder and magical appearance as he travels on, but eventually the pleasant dream fades and he is alone again. He comes to realize that the train is only a train. Neely is eventually found and returned to his mother's berth.

In the berth, Neely can now only wonder when they are going to arrive at wherever they are going so he can get off the train. The magic is dead, and even the remembrance of things past begins to fade away from his mind.

The tragic lost of a child's ability to see magic and happiness in everyday things is the theme of this story, coupled with the idea that parents unconsciously help in this disillusionment as they force their child to grow up. Neely undergoes role conflict, and in the final analysis, he slips towards the adult demands of societal role. Neely's role is defined and the definition of the situation tells him that the magic of childhood dies at adulthood. To become an adult is to become a pragmatist who does not subscribe to the wonders of a child's magical view towards the world. Neely's dream of a world of magic is destroyed and replaced by the sensate directives of the adult world.

"Man to Beat" (1958)

Autobiographical in tone, "Man to Beat" captures Beaumont's love for racing cars; in real life, Beaumont often raced a Porsche at Palm Springs, California. Jackson

Lynch, the racer who drives a Porsche Spyder in the story, is Beaumont's autobiographical counterpart.

This story is the account of Ben Hollister. During a meeting with fellow race drivers, the theme of death is introduced early, and each driver in his own way has a secret agreement with death, but none know when the next race might be their last. They are not afraid of death, but they are afraid of losing, which to them is another death by degree. It is the challenge of living life fully that counts. Hollister has come to kill John Koenig, because he was responsible for Hollister's son's death three years earlier, and he plans to carry out his revenge by murdering him on the race track. Hollister is confronted by Koenig's wife, Margaret, who tells Hollister that she knows his plan. Margaret also exposes the myth of racing: men race automobiles because it is life itself, not sport; it is a life of challenge, competition, and winning, and for them losing is the same as dying inside.

The race that follows is one of the most precise and exacting descriptions of race car driving found anywhere in contemporary literature; Beaumont puts the reader in the driver's seat and shows us what it is all about.

Hollister has his revenge by beating Koenig in the race rather than killing him; by losing, Koenig suffers death in a symbolic manner. Hollister plans to go on winning against Koenig until all parts of Koenig are truly beaten and dead, leaving behind only a mechanized husk of a man to walk through the motions of existence. To destroy Koenig's dream of winning is to destroy Koenig himself, and to destroy Koenig in this fashion becomes the dream of Hollister. Death, pursuit and destruction of a dream, possession of a dream, social masks, and role conflict are all major themes in this tense story.

"A World of Differents" (1958)

One of Beaumont's humorous stories, "A World of Differents" concerns an alien from Zaras who crashlands its craft on Earth, and attempts telepathic communication with earthlings. The alien fails in its effort to learn the English language from reading James Joyce's *Finnegans Wake*. Mistaken for an abandoned baby, the alien knows it must escape to survive; it plans to flee its crib, turn on the gas-heater, and blow up its human captors and their home.

Alone, the alien will seek shelter in the world outside the crib, and it realizes that its dream of communication with earthlings is lost. Outside of its crib, in the wild, the alien will probably perish.

This story is written in the vein of James Joyce's *Finnegans Wake*, and the the stream-of-consciousness writing technique mimics Joyce with uncanny accuracy. The alien gives the reader a perspective on the human condition that is both amusing and sad, and it is evident that the alien can hardly wait to get away from its human contamination and imprisonment.

The fact that Charles Beaumont enjoyed all forms of literature is reflected in this take-off on James Joyce. "A World of Differents" is James Joyce recreated and reinterpreted by Charles Beaumont as only Beaumont could achieve it.

"The New People" (1958)

A study in deviance, "The New People" is the story of a Certified Public Accountant named Hank Prentice, his wife, Ann, and their adopted son, Davey. Hank is sexually impotent, and although he and Ann have not consummated their marriage, they live together as husband and wife and have an adopted son. They are the new people on the block and have moved into a house where fifty people have committed suicide. They have been in the unusual house for three weeks, and the neighbors are having a housewarming party for them.

Matt Dystal secretly meets Hank after the party to tell him about the mysterious history of the strange house they have moved into, and confides that the neighbors have group activities together that are deadly to outsiders, especially those deemed unadaptable; these meetings give the group its thrills and alleviate their boredom. Currently, the neighbors are involved in Satanic Mass rituals. Too late, Hank realizes that his drink has been drugged; he watches in horror as his wife, Ann, becomes the virgin sacrifice.

Much later, the Prentice family will be disposed of, and once again the house will be sold to another party—the new people on the block. Throughout the plot, Hank is oftentimes at odds with his surroundings to one degree or another, but by the time he finally realizes the situation is not what it seems and there is more to his neighbors than he has imagined, it is too late for him and his family.

What is ethical and good becomes non-ethical, and evil is accepted as moral. Deviance is in the eyes of the beholder, and in this case, the definition of the situation is provided by the neighbors who hold social power; those in power control the situation and define what is normal and what is deviant. As a result, the newcomers become sacrificial societal victims and are displaced by the will of their neighbors.

"Perchance to Dream" (1958)

Philip Hall, age thirty-one, is a lonely man suffering from a cardiac condition; he seeks psychiatric help because he is afraid to fall asleep.

He confesses he is afraid to sleep for fear he will never wake up. He dreams, and his dreams become his reality. Currently, he is dreaming about a lovely young woman with whom he rides a roller coaster; he knows she brings death and stays awake to avoid the final dream where he will embrace her and then plunge from the roller coaster to the ground. There is a knock at the door and the receptionist enters; the psychiatrist introduces her as Miss Thomas. Hall recognizes her as the woman in his dream—Death's handmaiden. In a wild frenzy to escape her, he trips and falls out of the window, plunging thirteen floors to the concrete below, where he dies. But all is an illusion, and in a twist ending to this complex plot, the psychiatrist informs the receptionist that the young man has died of a heart attack. Only a minute had passed since Hall had entered the psychiatrist's office, sat down, fallen asleep, screamed, and died.

Life is an illusion, and the dream is the reality. In Hall's particular case, the dream kills. In the Jungian landscape of "Perchance to Dream," the sociological theme of paradoxical perception controls all aspects of the situation. Hall's ethnocentrism is seen on a more subtle level as valid, because he knows intuitively that his dreams are real and his belief in their validity is unshakeable; that the dream kills him substantiates his belief. A study in conflicting selves, this story has its roots in such works as *Monsieur Teste* by Paul Valéry (1871-1945), in which a character represents pure mind; "A Note on Illusion" by Oscar Wilde (1854-1900), which deals with social masks; and *Outward Bound* by Sutton Vane (1888-1963), which deals with experiences beyond death; and other examples of a similar nature which are also concerned with the illusion and reality found in the labyrinth of the unconscious mind.

"Miss Gentibelle" (1957)

A dark fantasy concerning a mother-son relationship, "Miss Gentibelle" is a creative variation of the theme found in Robert Bloch's novel, *Psycho*; it reveals the destructive side of parental love. The story opens with a young boy dressed in a girl's nightgown sitting in a tree watching his mother; his name is Robert. His mother, Miss Gentibelle, calls him to bed. Miss Gentibelle calls Robert by the name of Roberta because she wants him to see himself as a young girl. Robert tears his gown getting down from the tree, and as punishment, his mother kills his pet parakeet, named Margaret, with a butcher knife. Robert seeks solace and conversation with Mr. Drake Franklin, who lives in the house; later, Franklin leaves, promising to return for Robert. The mother says Franklin will not do as he said; she tells Robert to think and behave like a girl and to be her daughter rather than her son. Miss Gentibelle tells him that men are animals and not human beings. Later, she kills his pet frog with a knife, and Robert in turn uses a knife to kill her. The story concludes as Franklin returns to take Robert away from the madness he has known through Miss Gentibelle, a lonely woman with broken dreams.

The thin line between fantasy and reality is strikingly depicted throughout the story, and the sociological theme of paradoxical perception is evident as Robert attempts to sort through what is illusion and what is reality. Role conflict takes on a horrifying aspect in the plot, and shows what the mother seeks as her role and what Robert seeks as his role in his confused state.

Looking-glass self—the sociological theory that a child develops an image of himself only by finding out what other people think of him by using other people as a mirror to discover what he is like—finds Robert lost between the identity he should have and the one his mother desires for him.

"The Trigger" (1959)

"The Trigger" opens on a series of suicides. Philip Ives, working out of the Homicide Division of the San Francisco Police Department, is assigned to investigate these deaths. Role, identity, loneliness, social mask, pursuit of a dream, and death are the themes of this story. Each suicide has seemingly been a happy, contented male before his unexpected death.

Ives is a lonely man and a widower; his ambition and dream of solving every case he comes into contact with had indirectly kept him away from his wife the night she had been unable to reach help—he blames himself for his wife's subsequent death. This is brought into his consciousness during an investigative conversation with the club's bartender, Mr. Morrow. Morrow, who works at the elite club known as The Sportsman's Haven, had known each of the wealthy suicides. While leaving the establishment, Ives is almost run over and killed by a vehicle while dwelling on his own wife's death. At this point, the pieces of the puzzle start to come together, and Ives concludes the suicides were actually clever murders of the mind.

Ives returns to Morrow and tells him that within each human heart there is a special trigger of death, which that person pulls when someone or something forces him to destroy himself: something within the individual's mind causes him to seek self-destruction. Morrow, jealous of the wealthy patrons he meets in his inferior role as bartender, has discovered the hidden weaknesses within each of his victims, and his dream to eliminate them by triggering that weakness has been successful—he has turned his victims' minds inward to dwell upon their horrifying shortcomings until they are driven to the final act—suicide. Ives tells Morrow that he will frame him for murder in some manner, and Morrow, fearing failure, begins to dwell on the consequences thereof, and eventually commits suicide himself. The case is closed and Ives moves on to other murders.

"The Music of the Yellow Brass" (1959)

This story concerns Juanito Galvez and his encounter with the lovely woman, Andree, with the bull ring and bullfighting serving as a backdrop. Andree is the sexual image of the bull in the ring, with young Galvez as the bullfighter who must pierce her with his sword, which in this instance represents the penis symbol. In a parallel but unrelated creative manner, this image is similar to the one Ernest Hemingway employed in his novel *The Sun Also Rises* (1926), in which Lady Brett Ashley serves a similar role with her male onlookers. Galvez does seduce Andree, and during a night of wild sexual abandon and enjoyment, he does satisfy both their sexual needs; he overcomes the death image of Andree by piercing it with his being. By surviving the sexual encounter with Andree, Galvez imagines himself a potentially great matador with style despite the dire warnings of his companion, Enrique Cordoba. He will now face the bull in the ring, and as he conquered Andree, so he will conquer the bull.

98

There is little doubt in the reader's mind as Galvez steps into the bull ring that the bull will gore him to death and that Galvez will die in the sand. Technically, the woman is the handmaiden to death, and death is the bull; the woman represents illusion and the bull represents reality.

An ethnic study, "The Music of the Yellow Brass" displays a universality in in its depiction of the role of a young man and what is expected of him. Insightful as to what a man's role should be in a sensate setting, it reveals, too, that often men play false roles to secure both a personal and social definition of role among their peers and the members of the opposite sex. Galvez is an example of child-man in search of adulthood and role; he dies before he achieves them. Alone in his confrontation with the bull, Galvez will perish pursuing his dream of becoming a great matador.

"Sorcerer's Moon" (1959)

This story concerns two warlocks in conflict. Carnaday and Farrow both seek to become the most powerful warlock alive. A magical rune is given by Farrow to Carnaday, and Carnaday must get rid of the rune within three days or meet his death. Carnaday hires a detective named Mr. Bryan to deliver the rune to Farrow before the appointed time. Mr. Bryan does this and returns with a receipt for his services; on his way out of the door, Carnaday realizes he has been tricked, and the receipt in the envelope is the rune he tried to return to Farrow.

Alone, Carnaday stares in horror at the moon outside his window as midnight of the appointed day arrives. He knows he has lost the game and is no longer in control of the situation.

This is a morality tale of conflict interest groups. Each character is in conflict with the other over a defined interest. Carnaday is eliminated, Farrow achieves his goal, and Mr. Bryan is absorbed and accomodated into Farrow's goal by ensuring its fulfillment.

Each character at different points in the story controls the definition of the situation, but it is Carnaday who misinterprets it through paradoxical perception, and is destroyed by the illusion. Roles are affected accordingly. The rune is the key to distinction, and it gives at the same instant that it takes away. As a materialistic representation of success in the world of American business, the rune is the perfect American symbol: everything is written down on paper.

"The Howling Man" (1959)

Narrated by David Ellington, who is Charles Beaumont's disguised Everyman, this is an account of a man's encounter with Satan, and Brother Jerome and Brother Christophorus of St. Wulfran's Abbey in Europe. Given refuge from a storm by the kindly monks, David discovers the howling man locked away in captivity. Satan convinces Ellington that Brother Jerome is insane and has imprisoned him unfairly because his lifestyle is different from that of the monk's. Ellington sets free the man, who immediately transforms himself into Satan and vanishes. Within a short passage of time, World War Two erupts. Knowing the loneliness of a man who has committed an unpardonable error, Ellington's dream becomes an obsession to capture the howling man during his lifetime. Ellington grows older, and one day a card arrives from Brother Christophorus advising him that the howling man has been captured and imprisoned again. The greater dream of world peace and universal harmony is restored and once again intact. Ellington can relax and live out his life fully, secure in the knowledge that Satan has been confined.

The concept of good and the concept of evil are examined in this story, and the themes of role, pursuit of a dream, death, and loneliness are interwoven into the fabric of the plot. Although altered in some areas for its presentation on *The Twilight Zone* television series, "The Howling Man's" message and theme are essentially the same in visual impact; however, Beaumont is known to have resented the substitution of a staff for the Holy Cross in the TV production. Charles Beaumont was deeply religious man who saw the cross as the true symbol with which fight evil. As a religious and philosophical fiction work, "The Howling Man" is important because it reveals Beaumont as the Christian Existentialist he became; and because of that fact, it is a story that every scholar should read when analyzing his writings.

"Buck Fever" (1960)

"Buck Fever" is one of Charles Beaumont's most powerful stories. The message here is: it is all right to kill something if its death will show one how to live life in a more humane or meaningful manner, but it is immoral to kill out of blood lust. A story of social and personal masks, it is also an intricate study of role in the American business world.

George Ransome, Paul Arents, and Nathan Colby are deer hunting on a rainy, chilly October morning; it is their sixth day out without a kill. Colby is there to prove he fits into the ethical structure of Ransome and Arents's business world. On a subtle level, Colby, too, is running from the hunter and is being stalked. Colby must kill a deer to ensure his passage through the initiation rites demanded by the other two men. He does wound a deer, but when told to finish the animal off, he refuses. Colby realizes he will be considered a failure by the other two men, and that his career is finished. The two hunters depart, leaving Colby alone with his shattered dream of fitting into their business world as an equal. Gently, he strokes the deer's coat, then puts the animal out of its misery by shooting it. Colby then smashes his rifle against a tree and hurls the weapon into the dark brush. Later, he returns to camp and knows his true dream of being his own man is intact. He knows, too, that his wife Maureen will be waiting home for him when he returns; her love and understanding are part of his real dream, and he has not lost either during the hunting trip.

Through the death of the innocent deer, the innocent Colby lives on and his true dream is finally realized. He has also regained his spirit and his manhood; his loneliness is displaced. Colby has survived the hunt, and he has created meaning for himself out of a purposeless universe.

"Song for a Lady" (1960)

The setting for this story is an old ocean liner named the *Lady Anne*. The tale concerns the lives of a young American couple, Alan and Eileen Ransome. They board the disintegrating liner and find that it is full of elderly passengers, mostly Britishers in their seventies and eighties. The Ransomes are informed that their passage on the *Lady Anne* is a mistake, and at one point are offered a large sum of money to leave the ship prior to sailing. The couple refuses. The ship ultimately sails, and the Ransomes learn about the ship's history, coming to realize that it was originally intended for young honeymooners.

Some of the original honeymooners have returned for this special farewell reunion voyage, since the once proud luxury liner is finally to be retired from service. The *Lady Anne* represents the grace, manners, and traditions of a lost era, and it has a positive effect on the roles of Alan and Eileen as a married couple who have grown somewhat apart as individuals. They have become just another couple of human beings trying to survive in a technological society. Alan and Eileen rediscover themselves, and each other, during the cruise; they make love and become closer as a couple with their shared dreams and shared desires.

Near Cherbourg, the Ransome couple is put off by Captain Protheroe at gunpoint. They are told that a rescue ship will pick them up directly. In the lifeboat with their luggage and life jackets, the young couple watch as the contented, happy elderly couples wave pleasant goodbyes to them. The *Lady Anne* moves away and within a short time it sinks, taking its elderly passengers to a watery grave for their final interment.

The elderly couples welcome death with their dreams intact and with no fear of loneliness; the American couple face life with their rediscovered dream intact and with no fear of loneliness. This story examines the concepts of love and the pursuit of a dream.

"The Neighbors" (1960)

This tense story opens with Miles Cartier looking out the window holding a pistol in his left hand. Miles is defending himself from someone who wants to kill him and to destroy his dream of happiness with his family and career. The Cartier family—Miles, Sally, and their five-and-a-half-year-old son Jimmy—are black. They are being threatened by their white neighbors in Lakeside Heights. Miles cannot understand why ordinary Americans just like himself desire his death simply because the color of his skin is black. The confrontation comes, but it is not what Miles expected. A man named Jensen and others come to his home, and with them is Arnold March.

Miles drops his pistol on the couch and faces the assembled group. March confesses it was he and he alone who has been responsible for every act against the newly arrived black family. Jensen makes it plain to Miles that March will be turned over to the police, and requests that Miles give the neighborhood and the neighbors another chance. Miles is invited to the weekly ritual of poker playing with the white men, and knows he will not have to move from the neighborhood. The Miles Cartier family have found a home in a good neighborhood where brotherhood and friendship is still possible.

The dream of brotherhood and its pursuit is evident in this story, and reflects Beaumont's theme that no matter what color or ethnic group an individual derives from, that individual is still a human being and should be treated as something other than a stereotype. The concept of brotherhood and understanding is interwoven around the themes of death, pursuit of a dream, role, and loneliness.

Although a very short work, "The Neighbors" deals with what it means to be different and the effect of being different upon individuality. The story places emphasis on the individual's inescapable solidarity with his or her fellow human beings.

"The Magic Man" (1960)

This poetic story was one of Beaumont's personal favorites as well as being an ever popular story among his readers. It is filled with rich imagery and color, almost every paragraph coming alive with its intense beauty. "The Magic Man" tells the tale of a dying Everyman who has learned the tricks of survival.

Dr. Silk travels the countryside in a wagon pulled by mules; he is called The Magic Man, and he performs wonders and magic for his audiences. His traveling companion is a black man named Obadiah. Together, they cross the prairies, prime the crowds, and sell a harmless liquid medicine called "Doctor Silk's Wonderol." They arrive in Two Forks and Dr. Silk opens for business. He proves again that he is a master showman and magician, charming the eager crowd and entertaining them.

Silk is a master of illusion, but believes that life itself is more magical than any trick he could ever perform; to show his love and gratitude to the crowd, he decides to explain how his tricks work. Unwell, Dr. Silk wants others to realize that true magic is everywhere—inside one's head, in the wonder of nature—and he wants to share this wonderful secret. The crowd's interest dies, and it leaves, realizing Dr. Silk is just an ordinary person with no special powers. Alone, Dr. Silk feels the pains in his body again and senses that he is dying, but takes comfort in the thought he has shared his dream of magic and dispelled the loneliness of the moment. Finished, Dr. Silk and Obadiah pack up the wagon and travel on, leaving Two Forks, Kansas, behind forever.

A study in role expectations, "The Magic Man" also examines the importance of having a dream to share with others in a lonely world; to share that particular dream before death, with feeling, is to be remembered. Whether one is remembered for shattering the dream or for expanding the beauty and magic of the dream is secondary to the act of sharing it with others as an act of love. An act of love can and does take courage.

"Gentlemen, Be Seated" (1960)

This philosophical story examines the loneliness created by the loss of humor. It is the story of James Kinkaid and his confrontation with William Agnew Biddle, his superior at Spears's Research Laboratory. Biddle feels there may yet be hope for Kinkaid and attempts to make him into a true human being who can laugh. Kinkaid is first taken to a restaurant called Kelly's where Kinkaid encounters some new sensations of dining. Then he is taken to a strange place in No Man's Land where everything revolves around gags and madcap humor; he is confused and terrified by the chilling experience. It is here that Kinkaid is advised that he is being considered for membership in the Society for the Preservation of Laughter. But laughter is something Kinkaid is afraid of, for he has been reared in a technological culture where laughter is a dead subject. Kinkaid fails the tests for initiation and membership, and the following morning, he is fired from his position at Spears's Research Laboratory. During the long, lonely nights ahead, he will continue his search for the lovely sound of laughter in the dying hope that he can share in the dream of the Society for the Preservation of Laughter.

This is a sad, depressing look at a world without laughter and a world without dreams. The hint of death hovers over the character of Kinkaid as his role confusion intensifies, for without rediscovering what he has lost, he will eventually die; he must find his lost humanity in the subtleties of laughter. Having lost his ability to laugh, he must search out its identifying sound or perish in the attempt. This is one of Beaumont's most sophisticated, philosophical pieces, and it showcases Beaumont's ability as a keen social critic of the contemporary American scene.

"The Baron's Secret" (1960)

Written in the form of a chronicle, this is the curious account of of an Englishman lost in Germany's Black Forest. He chances upon the abode of a German Baron and is invited into the Baron's castle. The Baron and his beautiful wife prove to be a charming couple, and their abode a fascination for the lost traveler. The Englishman no longer feels alone.

The traveler falls under the spell of the beautiful Baroness and discovers himself sexually aroused. The Baron promises to take the traveler to the railway in the morning, and the evening of good company and lively conversation comes to an end. Later during the storm-filled night, the Baroness comes to the traveler and they spend the night together engaged in passionate lovemaking; satiated, the Baroness departs, and the traveler falls into a deep sleep, his sexual desires satisfied beyond his wildest dreams. Morning comes, and the Baron and the traveler depart for the railway; they ride flame-red stallions to the village. Prior to departure, a conversation ensues, and the Baron confesses that he had found his wife making love to a chance guest some six months previously, and had then ordered the guest away, murdering his wife with his bare hands. This comes as a chilling shock to the traveler and he quickly boards the train and departs.

For years afterwards, the Englishman cannot hear the phrase "laying a ghost" to rest without going into hysterics. His friends liken his moods to Sydenham's chorea and fantods.

A study in social masking and role, this story also conveys the themes of death, pursuit of a dream, and loneliness. Charles Beaumont wrote this story under his pseudonym of Michael Phillips.

106

"Dead You Know" (1960)

This is the bizarre account of Diggory Sprool's enjoyment of killing his wife Emma once a week. At the age of thirteen, Sprool had decided to become an artist, and commenced making clay heads; a lonely man, he continues this vocation into adulthood. But his dream is shattered by loss of money, marriage to Emma Hurlburt, and a reduced station in life, all of which force him to take a position as a freight dispatcher (much as Beaumont himself did at the time of his own marriage). Over a period of time, his hate for his slothful, indolent wife takes the form of a weekly ritual of modeling her in clay and then performing atrocities upon the graven image. Returning home while whistling a melody from Mendelssohn, he immediately seeks out his latest Emma masterwork to abuse it; although the visit to his employer, Mr. Fish, had interrupted his evening, he is now free to enjoy himself.

He destroys his latest model by shooting arrows into it, not abandoning his bow until the latest Emma masterwork resembles a fat pincushion. Later, he searches for the real Emma and discovers that she has been killed while sitting behind the chair holding the Emma statuary. He flees to Rio de Oro and takes up with a charming Spanish girl; she poses for him, and the dream of becoming a great artist is once again found and reawakened. Unfortunately, the girl's husband returns one night and kills Sprool with a long machette, thus ending the second attempt at an artistic career by Diggory Sprool.

Role conflict, pursuit of a dream, loneliness, death and dying, frustrated sexuality, and social masking are the major themes in this mystery story. Sprool seeks to kill the clay image—the masked husk—of Emma, and eventually the husk is penetrated and the real Emma dies; the arrow becomes a complex penis symbol and the bow its silent deliverer. Sprool symbolizes the frustrated artist struggling against a sensate society, his dream destroyed by his own inabilities.

107

"Blood Brother" (1961)

The future setting for this story is an active sensate culture that includes vampires. Mr. Smith has gone to a psychiatrist seeking to cure himself of the fate which has befallen him: he has become a vampire, and he finds that he is having a difficult time keeping a day job. He continually falls asleep during the daylight hours, and his nights must remain free to allow him to roam and hunt. This too reminds him that he is out of step with the acceptable social standards of the day world. He has tried to tell himself that he is a human being first and a vampire second, but it is becoming increasingly difficult for him to relate to the regular norms of the living. After listening to the young man and asking probing questions, the psychiatrist declares that he has a cure for Mr. Smith's problem.

The psychiatrist picks up a mahogany letter opener and buries it to the hilt in Mr. Smith's heart. Directly, the psychiatrist calls Dorcas on the telephone—the woman who had originally bitten Mr. Smith on the neck and then suggested that he contact the psychiatrist—and says to the party on the line to tell Dorcas that it is her fiancé calling. He waits for Dorcas, idly scratching the two vampire marks on his neck which Dorcas gave him. The psychiatrist is at ease with his role, for in a technological society he is the ultimate high priest.

In the case of social deviance, those in power who control the definition of the situation will define what is normal and abnormal for everyone else. One dream is shared by everyone in this lonely landscape, and anyone daring to assert his or her individuality is terminated. One may only pursue a dream if it is acceptable to the masses. These are the subtle messages in this story. The vampire is symbolic of a greater malaise.

"Something in the Earth" (1963)

Written before "Mourning Song," this chilling story reflects Charles Beaumont's fascination with the themes of death, loneliness, pursuit of a dream, individuality, role, and social mask. Beaumont would write only one major story after this one, "Mourning Song." Both tales are well-crafted, intact, and created as Beaumont's mental facilities started to depart him, leaving him with the intuition that he was soon to die. Beaumont also started his autobiography but did not live to complete it.

"Something in the Earth" is a poignant examination of a husband and wife watching their world die; their names are Gerald and Sylvan Markeson. The Earth has become polluted and highly technological; sensate ethics is the philosophical approach to living life, and preservation of the environment has been displaced to preserve the city. Yet something precious within the Earth refuses to die and struggles against the horrors humankind has committed against it. In a subtle sense, this can also be visualized as an intimate, personal struggle by Charles Beaumont against the Alzheimer's Disease which had begun destroying his mental faculties. Beaumont knew something was wrong with himself and he was refusing to give in to it; this story reflects his philosophical attempt to rebel and resist.

At the conclusion of the story, a miracle does take place, and in the final conflict between nature and man, nature displaces humankind. Markeson watches from one of his beloved treetops as civilization begins literally to crumble. Roots from the giant trees spread and topple the cities, and water floods the streets killing the people therein; the mountains pull the Earth apart and make room for the forests and the fields that have displaced the cancer known as humanity.

"Mourning Song" (1963)

"Mourning Song" was Charles Beaumont's last written story, and it is one of the author's finest mainstream fiction creations, taking its place alongside that of "Black Country." "Mourning Song" contains many of the same themes that Beaumont wrote about throughout his short career, and the central theme of death permeates the structure of this complex story. This is the account of an old blind man named Solomon from Hunter's Hill; when he plays the mourning song on his guitar, the individual the song is directed to dies within a short period of time, for there is no way to run from the hunter and Solomon is Death personified. Solomon is a contemporary Pied Piper of Hamlin: his mourning song touches everybody sooner or later, and there is no escaping it.

Narrated by a young man, Lonnie Younger, "Mourning Song" deliberately contrasts the two characters, displaying: rashness versus wisdom, the passions of youth versus the infirmities of old age, rebellion versus acceptance, sexuality versus impotence, will versus defeat, shadow versus illusion and vice versa, the new versus the old, the young and healthy versus old and dying, the companionship of youth versus the loneliness of old age, the social mask versus the naked face, and the untarnished dream versus the shattered dream. The plot traces Younger's life from age eleven through age twenty-four, and shows the effect of Solomon's presence on the community.

Younger plans to marry the lovely Etilla. One day, Solomon plays the mourning song for him; Younger rebels, but the community rejects him as already dead. Younger chokes Solomon to death in anger before thirty witnesses and is arrested for murder by Sheriff Crowder. The dream of possessing Etilla and all that she symbolizes is replaced by the nightmare of Solomon and all that he symbolizes. Younger hears and sees Solomon from the prison window, knowing that his murder trial is set for the following day.

NOTE: Five stories written by Beaumont earlier in his career were first published posthumously in 1988, and are covered below.

"To Hell with Claude" (1988)

A previously unpublished story co-authored with Chad Oliver, this is the third and final tale of Claude Adams, three times the father of Earth's population. Claude finds that he has failed to destroy fantasy, or anything else connected with it, such as imagination and dreaming. Old and in poor health, Claude must do something to change the course of human events before he dies, and his civilization begins to self-destruct. Adams goes to Arkham, Massachusetts, where he encounters the worshipers of the Lovecraftian god Cthulhu, including: Dr. Nameless, Professor Monk Lewis, catacombs, Karl Marx, and others. In this off-beat satire Adams's companion Cleve becomes a naked Eve. As the story concludes, Earth is again destroyed, and it begins raining strawberries. For the Earth to be reborn and start anew, it must once again become aborted. Claude goes off with Eve to start over again.

There are several themes running through this satire, including: decay and death, loneliness, alienation, the outsider, and individuality. Despite the overall feeling of world-weariness, "To Hell With Claude" succeeds very well as satiric humor.

"Appointment with Eddie" (1988)

"Eddie" is the story of thirty-six-year-old Shecky King. King is an exceedingly successful show business performer; he joins George at a local bar, questioning whether he is actually a success. King decides that he must visit Eddie the Barber in Endsburg, and George accompanies him on the journey. King pleads with George to make an

111

appointment with the barber. Eddie the Barber is the personification of decay, old age, and death. Eddie tells George that no amount of money can buy a haircut for King, because he does not have an opening in his schedule. King confronts Eddie and is turned away. As the plot unfolds, George comes to learn that a haircut from Eddie means success in life for the person receiving it! However successful a person then became, Eddie could cancel that success if he made the decision to do so; where or not this happened depended upon what kind of success a person pursued and how that success was utilized and realized. The story concludes with King committing suicide and George thanking God that George is bald. Either King was undeserving of the haircut of success, took the place of another who rightfully deserved the haircut, betrayed the gift of success, or a combination of all three.

The theme of death and decay permeates this story. A sense of loneliness fills the fabric of the story and touches all its characters. A dark, brooding story, "Appointment with Eddie" focuses successfully upon the question, "What price success?" We also see Charles Beaumont's enduring themes of death, decay, and suicide.

"The Crime of Willie Washington" (1988)

The story opens with Willie Washington stabbing George Manassan in the stomach. Manassan survives. Washington had attacked Manassan because of what he had said about Washington's wife, Cleota. Later, Washington is mistakenly accused of the rape and murder of a woman and is sentenced to die for his supposed crime. He is innocent, a fact which seems to be confirmed by a curious event: attempts to hang him suddenly fail. He is released from prison, and learns that his wife has run off with another man. Washington is unable to find employment. Depressed, he contemplates suicide; yet, at the final moment, he overcomes his hatred and loneliness, and returns to his Aunt Lucy, his only true friend. Together, they share coffee and laugh together. The themes of death and

112

decay, loneliness, alienation, and suicide are evident in this short work, a previously unpublished story written prior to 1963.

"The Man with the Crooked Nose" (1988)

This is the strange story of Martin Gershenson, who works in a bookstore. Gershenson has the wonderful gift of being able to hum the major musical works of the world. He one day encounters a mysterious man named John S. Parker, whom he recognizes from his days in a Nazi Concentration Camp. Gershenson leaves the store and never returns, taking with him his beautiful gift of musical expression. The structure of the story points directly to the themes of loneliness, death and decay, and illusion versus reality. Gershenson is an indirect literary reference to one of Charles Beaumont's favorite American composers, George Gershwin (1898-1937) who wrote *Rhapsody in Blue* in 1924; Gershwin, a musical genius, died at the height of his creative powers of a brain tumor. Charles Beaumont was also able to whistle themes from any musical masterpiece that he fancied. "The Man with the Crooked Nose" includes autobiographical overtones and also touches on the use of imagination and fantasy to survive one's everyday existence.

"The Carnival" (1988)

"The Carnival," like "To Hell with Claude," "Appointment with Eddie," "The Crime of Willie Washington," and "The Man with The Crooked Nose," first appeared in *Charles Beaumont: Selected Stories* in 1988. Edited by Roger Anker, the book won the prestigious Bram Stoker Award.

"The Carnival" is vintage Charles Beaumont. The writing is sharp, magical, and has an intense beauty all its own; it ranks among Beaumont's best writing. Set in the month of October, it is the poignant story of Lars Nielson

113

In the actual universe of his existence, Lars is a sixteen-year-old male confined to a wheelchair, but in the absolute universe, Lars's imagination allows him to control his feeling. He is taken to a carnival by his father. Along the way, he undergoes scenes that induce an hallucinogenic feeling within him of keen intensity. The story concludes with Lars becoming one with his inner world of imagination and eventually going insane. For the rest of his crippled existence Lars will see things from the magical eyes of a young boy riding on a fantasy bicycle!

This metaphysical adventure, one of Beaumont's greatest short works, can be enjoyed on several levels of interpretation. A carnival is an excellent symbol for death and decay. Beaumont's unique tale stands well beside such carnival settings as the classic *Something Wicked this Way Comes* by Ray Bradbury, *City of Baraboo* by Barry B. Longyear, and other noted writings by authors who have utilized the carnival/circus setting within the framework of a story, poem, novel, or play. For Beaumont, fantasy and imagination are sometimes the last strongholds against the coming of that wicked darkness which destroys the mind—perhaps, it is Beaumont himself who intuits the darkness approaching to steal his mind. He fights it while he can. To endure, to last just a little while longer, to create, to struggle before becoming overcome by darkness, all of these were important in the writer's life and work. Another theme in this unusual story is the subtle idea that escaping one's body can be another form of magic. Escape the body before you are brain dead; escape the body before it betrays you; escape the body before it hurts you; escape the body by entering that magical doorway to another dimension before your mind forgets who and what it is and was and once dreamed. Those readers interested in Vedanta and Tibetan Buddhism should discover some complex insights in "The Carnival." To escape one's body *is* magic.

With the passage of time, Charles Beaumont's "The Carnival" will be seen by readers and critics alike as one of his greatest creations—the true mark of a first-rate writer with the gift and ability to create lasting works of literature for future readers and future writers of fiction. All of Beaumont's themes are present in "The Carnival," some becoming variations of others, intertwining and producing a work that reveals everything that is great about Charles Beaumont.

IX.

CONCLUSION

The legacy of Charles Beaumont is assured in the genre of American fantasy literature, both for his direct influence on the styles and themes of many of the writers working today, and for his vivid and honest characterizations of ordinary people thrown into extraordinary situations. Beaumont would have been successful in any genre, and in fact proved himself adept at moving from pulp fiction to slick fiction to nonfiction to television and film writing. His preference for the fantasy category in most of these forms possibly reflects his escapist reading as a child and his interest in the versatility of this genre as once-removed social commentary. Fantasy is also the hardest of the fiction categories in which to create believable situations and characters.

Beaumont's work helped shatter editorial taboos in the mid-1950s, making possible the further exploration of controversial themes by later writers. His sophisticated style helped integrate the fantasy literature of the pulps into mainstream American fiction, particularly in such magazines as *Playboy*. He also foresaw that a technologically-oriented society would foster a widespread lack of interpersonal communication and enhance the possibility of role conflict between individuals.

Beaumont was a singer of words, and his prose literally dances with life. To read "My Grandmother's Japonicas" or "Good Lord, It's Alive!" or "The Carnival," "The Howling Man," "The Music of the Yellow Brass," "Mourning Song," or *The Intruder* for the first time is a unique experience, one the reader will never forget. The magic of these words is also evident in the legendary tele-

116

plays he created for Rod Serling's TV series, *The Twilight Zone*. Among the noteworthy scripts that he penned for this groundbreaking series are: "The Howling Man," adapted from his short story of the same name, first shown on November 4, 1960; "Perchance to Dream," first shown on November 27, 1959; "In His Image," first shown on January 3, 1963; "Long Live Walter Jameson," first aired on March 18, 1960; "Miniature," first shown on February 21, 1963; and "Passage on the *Lady Ann*," first aired on May 9, 1963. Rerun endlessly since their first appearance, these and the other teleplays and screenplays that he wrote for the small and large screen remain just as vital and entertaining today as they were three decades ago.

Beaumont was also a master of creating believable dialogue—dialogue which is still studied and analyzed by beginning script writers today for its clarity, richness, subtle irony, and realism. His death at so young an age deprived American letters of a writer who could have become another John Steinbeck, Saul Bellow, or William Faulkner. A happy, family-oriented man with a zest for living and enjoying friendships, Beaumont died as bizarrely as any of his fictional creations. In the Summer of 1963 his friends noticed that the thirty-four-year-old author was suddenly looking much older than his years, and was beginning to have memory and personality problems. After a myriad of tests, he was diagnosed with a rare form of early Alzheimer's disease. Soon he was institutionalized, his extraordinary intelligence completely gone, and his physical faculties rapidly failing. He died on February 21, 1967, just a month past his thirty-eighth birthday. Yet, although active as a writer for little more than a decade, Charles Beaumont left a literary legacy that will endure and be read and studied for generations to come.

This analytical study is offered as a beginning place for Beaumont scholars, in the hope that it will spark additional commentary and further insights—sociological, literary, philosophical—into the life and work of a writer who will live for all time. How do I know? Beaumont himself told me so in "The Magic Man":

He knew they would believe him. After all,
how can you doubt the word of a man who
pulls roses out of the air?

PRIMARY BIBLIOGRAPHY

by William F. Nolan

NOTE: For a comprehensive bibliography of Beaumont's works, see *The Work of Charles Beaumont: An Annotated Bibliography & Guide, Second Edition*, by William F. Nolan (Borgo Press, 1990).

FICTION BOOKS

The Hunger and Other Stories. New York: G. P. Putnam's Sons, April 1957. [collection]

Run from the Hunter (with John Tomerlin as Keith Grantland). Greenwich, CT: Fawcett Gold Medal Books, September 1957. [novel]

Yonder: Stories of Fantasy and Science Fiction. New York: Bantam Books, April 1958. [collection]

The Intruder. New York: G. P. Putnam's Sons, August 1959. [novel]

Night Ride and Other Journeys. New York: Bantam Books, March 1960. [collection]

The Magic Man—and Other Science Fantasy Stories. Greenwich, CT: Fawcett Gold Medal Books, April, 1965. [collection]

The Edge. London: Panther Books, 1966. [collection]

Best of Beaumont. Toronto, New York: Bantam Books, December 1982. [collection]

Charles Beaumont: Selected Stories, edited by Roger Anker. Arlington Heights, IL: Dark Harvest, August 1988. Reprinted as *The Howling Man*, New York: Tor, 1992. [collection]

NONFICTION BOOKS

Remember? Remember? New York: Macmillan, November 1963. [essay collection]

NONFICTION ANTHOLOGIES

Omnibus of Speed: An Introduction to the World of Motor Sport, co-edited with William F. Nolan. New York: G. P. Putnam's Sons, November 1958.

When Engines Roar, co-edited with William F. Nolan. Toronto, New York: Bantam Pathfinder, September 1964.

FICTION ANTHOLOGY

The Fiend in You, co-edited with William F. Nolan. New York: Ballantine Books, 1962.

SHORT FICTION APPEARANCES: MAGAZINES

Amazing Stories (1951); *Bachelor* (1958); *Collier's* (1957); *Esquire* (1955); *Gamma* (1963, 1965); *If: Worlds of Science Fiction* (1952, 1954, 1955); *Imagination* (1953, 1957); *Infinity* (1956); *The Magazine of Fantasy & Science Fiction* (1954, 1955, 1956, 1967); *Manhunt* (1959); *Nugget* (1956, 1960—both stories appeared under the pen name of Michael Phillips); *Orbit Science Fiction* (1953, 1954); *Playboy* (1954, 1955, 1956, 1957, 1958, 1959, 1961); *Road & Track* (1958, 1959); *Rogue* (1957, 1958, 1959, 1960—pen names employed include S. M. Tenneshaw, Michael Phillips, C. B. Lovehill); *The Saturday Evening Post* (1956); *Science Fiction Quarterly* (1954); *Sports Car Journal* (1957); *Terror Detective Story Magazine* (April, 1957, collaboration with William F. Nolan as "Frank Anmar"); *Universal-International News* (1952); *Venture Science Fiction* (1957).

ANTHOLOGY APPEARANCES: SELECTIVE TITLES

Best from Playboy, The Graveyard Reader, The Hollywood Nightmare, Masks, Acts of Violence, Treasury of Jazz, Social Problems Through Science Fiction, Taboo, Stories for the Dead of Night, Shock, Man Against Tomorrow, among many others.

NONFICTION APPEARANCES: MAGAZINES

Autosport (1957); *Carte Blanche* (1960, 1961); *Fortnight* (1955, 1956, 1957); *The Magazine of Fantasy & Science Fiction* (1955, 1956, 1957, 1959); *Playboy* (1955, 1959, 1960, 1961, 1962, 1963, 1965); *Rogue* (1956, 1957, 1959); *Show Business Illustrated* (1962); *Sports Cars Illustrated* (1959—an article concerning Charles Beaumont's experiences in racing).

NONFICTION APPEARANCES IN BOOKS

Masques, edited by J. N. Williamson. Baltimore: Maclay and Associates, 1984. This contains an autobiographical account of Charles Beaumont's childhood titled "My Grandmother's Japonicas." The book also carries a new tribute to Beaumont by Ray Russell, and reprints William F. Nolan's tribute, "Beaumont: The Magic Man." "My Grandmother's Japonica's" was later reprinted in the second edition of *The Work of Charles Beaumont: An Annotated Bibliography & Guide*, by William F. Nolan (San Bernardino, CA: The Borgo Press, 1990).

SCREENPLAYS

Queen of Outer Space (1958); *The Intruder* (adapted from the author's novel by Beaumont, 1962, and including an appearance by Beaumont as an actor in the film); *The Wonderful World of the Brothers Grimm* (1962); *Burn, Witch, Burn* (1962); *The Premature Burial* (1962); *The Haunted Palace* (1963); *The Seven Faces of Dr. Lao* (1964); *Masque of the Red Death* (1964); *Mister Moses* (1965).

SCRIPTS FOR TELEVISION

The Twilight Zone

"Perchance to Dream" (1959); "Elegy" (1960); "Long Live Walter Jameson" (1960); "A Nice Place to Visit" (1960); "The Howling Man" (1960); "Long Distance Call" (1961); "Static" (1961); "The Prime Mover" (1961); "Shadow Play" (1961); "The Jungle" (1961); "Dead Man's Shoes" (1962); "The Fugitive" (1962); "In His Image" (1963); "Valley of the Shadow" (1963); "Miniature" (1963); "Printer's Devil" (1963); "The New Exhibit" (1963); "Passage on the Lady Ann" (1963); "Number Twelve Looks Just Like You" (1964); "Queen of the Nile" (1964). Some of the later scripts were partially or wholly ghostwritten by Beaumont's friends to help provide for his family.

Other TV Programs

Beaumont did a great number of television scripts for different programs, and some in collaboration with William F. Nolan, George Clayton Johnson, Richard Matheson, Leonard Pruyn, OCee Ritch, Jerry Sohl, and John Tomerlin. Some of these television programs included *Four Star Playhouse; Wanted: Dead or Alive; Have Gun—Will Travel, Nemo, The D.A.'s Man, Philip Marlowe, Buckskin, Markham, One Step Beyond, Naked City, Channing, Thriller, Route 66, The Outlaws, Alfred Hitchcock Presents, Savage, The Racers, Cheyenne, Whodunit, Richard Diamond, Bulldog Drummond, Steve Canyon, Suspense, Climax*, among others.

COMIC BOOKS AND OTHERS

Charles Beaumont sold thirty scripts to Whitman Publications's Dell Comics line in the mid-1950s—ten of these in collaboration with William F. Nolan. Non-bylined, they appeared in *Mickey Mouse Comics*, *Donald Duck Comics*, *Walt Disney's Comics*, *Tweety and Sylvester Comics*, and *Woody Woodpecker Comics*. Beaumont was an assistant editor at Dell Comics during 1954. In 1948, as Charles McNutt, he illustrated an A. E. van Vogt collection, *Out of the Unknown*, for Fantasy Publishing Company; by 1950, he abandoned art for writing.

SECONDARY SOURCES

Allen, Reginald E. *Greek Philosophy: Thales to Aristotle.* New York: Free Press, 1966.

Barrett, William. *Irrational Man: A Study in Existential Philosophy.* Garden City, NY: Doubleday, 1958.

Becker, Ernest. *The Structure of Evil.* New York: Free Press, 1968.

Berger, Peter. *The Sacred Canopy.* Garden City, NY: Doubleday, 1964.

Berger, Peter, and Thomas Luckman. *The Social Construction of Reality.* Garden City, NY: Doubleday, 1966.

Bergson, Henri. *Creative Evolution.* New York: Modern Library, 1946.

Berkeley, George. *Three Dialogues between Hylas and Philonous.* edited by C. Turbayne. New York: Liberal Arts Press, 1954.

Blanshard, Brand. *The Nature of Thought.* London: Allen & Unwin, 1964.

Blau, Peter M. *Exchange and Power in Social Life.* New York: Wiley, 1964.

Blumer, Herbert. *Symbolic Interactionism: Perspective and Method.* Englewood Cliffs, NJ: Prentice-Hall, 1969.

Bottomore, Thomas B. *Sociology as Social Criticism.* London: George Allen & Unwin, 1974.

Bretall, Robert. *A Kierkegaard Anthology.* Princeton, NJ: Princeton University Press, 1951.

Burch, William R., Jr. *Daydreams and Nightmares: A Sociological Essay on the American Environment.* New York: Harper & Row, 1971.

Camus, Albert, all available writings.

Carritt, E. F. *The Theory of Morals.* New York: Oxford University Press, 1928.

Chambliss, Rollin. *Social Thought.* New York: Dryden, 1954.

Cicourel, Aaron. *Cognitive Sociology: Language and Meaning in Social Interaction.* New York: Free Press, 1974.

Cohen, Percy. *Modern Social Thought.* New York: Basic Books, 1968.

Collins, Randall. *Conflict Sociology: Toward an Explanatory Science.* New York: Academic Press, 1975.

Cooley, Charles Horton. *Human Nature and the Social Order.* New York: Schocken Books, 1964.

Coser, Lewis A. *The Functions of Social Conflict.* Glencoe: Free Press, 1956.

Dewey, John. *Human Nature and Conduct.* New York: Modern Library, 1930.

Duncan, H. D. *Symbols in Society,* New York: Oxford University Press, 1968.

Duncan, H. D. *Symbols and Social Theory.* New York: Oxford University Press, 1969.

Fromm, Erich. *Psychoanalysis and Religion.* New Haven: Yale University Press, 1950.

Fromm, Erich. *To Have or to Be.* New York: Harper & Row, 1976.

Ewing, A. C. *Ethics.* New York: Free Press, 1965.

Goffman, Erving. *Frame Analysis—An Essay on the Organization of Experiences.* Cambridge, MA: Harvard University Press, 1974.

Goffman, Erving. *Interaction Ritual.* Garden City, NY: Anchor Books, 1967.

Gusfield, Joseph. *Symbolic Crusade.* Urbana: University of Illinois Press, 1963.

Hughes, H. Stuart. *Consciousness and Society.* New York: Vintage, 1961.

James, William. *Essays in Pragmatic.* New York: Hafner, 1952.

Janowitz, Morris, ed. *William I. Thomason, Social Organization and Social Personality.* Chicago: University of Chicago Press, 1966.

Kierkegaard, Søren, *Fear and Trembling.* Garden City, NY: Anchor Books, 1954.

Kinloch, Graham C. *Sociological Theory: Its Development and Major Paradigms.* New York: McGraw-Hill, 1977.

Kirk, G. S., and J. E. Raven. *The Pre-Socratic Philosophers.* London: Cambridge University Press, 1957.

Larson, Calvin J. *Major Themes in Sociological Theory.* New York: David McKay, 1973.

Lerner, Daniel. *The Passing of Traditional Society.* New York: Free Press, 1958.

Martindale, Don. *The Nature and Types of Sociological Theory.* Boston: Houghton Mifflin, 1960.

Maslow, Abraham H. *Motivation and Personality.* New York: Harper & Row, 1970.

Matza, David. *Becoming Deviant.* Englewood Cliffs, N.J.: Prentice-Hall, 1969.

McClelland, David C. *The Achieving Society.* Princeton: Van Nostrand, 1961.

Mead, George Herbert. *Mind, Self, and Society,* edited and with an introduction by Charles W. Morris. Chicago: University of Chicago Press, 1934.

Mills, C. Wright. *The Sociological Imagination*. New York: Oxford University Press, 1959.

Montague, William P. *The Ways of Things*, Englewood Cliffs, NJ: Prentice-Hall, 1940.

Nietzsche, Friedrich. *The Portable Nietzsche*, edited by Walter Kaufmann. New York: Viking Press, 1959.

Nolan, William F. *The Work of Charles Beaumont: An Annotated Bibliography & Guide*. San Bernardino, CA: The Borgo Press, 1986; 2nd ed., 1990.

Nowell-Smith, P. *Ethics*. Baltimore, MD: Penguin Books, 1956.

Parson, Talcott. *Essays in Sociological Theory*. New York: Free Press, 1954.

Pears, D. F. *The Nature of Metaphysics*. New York: St. Martins Press, 1957.

Popkin, Richard H. *The History of Skepticism from Erasmus to Descartes*. New York: Harper & Row, 1968.

Rand, Benjamin. *Modern Classical Philosophers*. Boston: Houghton Mifflin, 1936.

Ross, David. *The Right and the Good*. Oxford, England: Clarendon Press, 1930.

INDEX

126

127

movie theatres, 32
Mussolini, Benito, 30
mystery and suspense writing, 14, 88
Naked City (TV show), 34
Nassau, Bahamas, 9
Nazi Germany, 113
New Orleans, Louisiana, 46
Nietzsche, Friedrich Wilhelm, 41
Nolan, William F., 7-8, 12-13, 15, 31, 34, 88, 119-122
nonconformity, 7, 16
Normand, Mabel, 32
North Hollywood, California, 7
nostalgia, 10, 17, 20-21
Nutt, Charles Hiram, 5, 14
Nutt, Charles Leroy (*i.e.*, Charles Beaumont), 6, 11, 14, *passim*
Nutt, Violet "Letty" Phillips, 5, 9, 14
Oboler, Arch, 30
Og, Son of Fire (radio), 30
Oliver, Chad, 12-13, 20, 22-23, 65, 74, 111, 113
One Step Beyond (TV), 34
Pal, George, 9, 13
Palm Springs, California, 92
Pan, god, 78
Panther Books, 11
Pathe-American, 10
Peanuts (cartoon), 30
Peter Quill (radio), 30
The Phantom (magazine), 31
Philips, Lee, 35
Phillips, Michael (*pseudonym* of Charles Beaumont), 106
Phillips, Violet—SEE: Nutt, Violet Phillips
Playboy, 7-9, 11, 15, 20-21, 51, 116
Poe, Edgar Allan, 10, 19, 36
Pogo (cartoon), 30
Popeye (cartoon), 30
Porsche automobile, 9, 92-93
The Premature Burial (film), 10, 36
Preminger, Otto, 9
Prince Valiant (cartoon), 30
Prosser, Lee, 135
Queen of Outer Space (film), 9, 36
racism, 8, 16, 38, 41-42, 103
radio, 6, 29-30
railroads and trains, 33, 47, 92
Randall, Tony, 11, 36

Reade, Charles, 40
Rhapsody in Blue (music by George Gershwin), 113
Richard Diamond (TV), 34
Ritch, OCee, 15, 34
Roberts, William, 36
Robin Hood, 74
Rogue, 8
"Rogue of Distinction" (column), 8
Rolland, Romain, 46
Roman procession, 46
Roosevelt, Franklin Delano, 30
Route 66 (TV show), 34
Russell, Ray, 10, 13, 20, 22-24, 36
San Diego Racing Circuit, 9
San Francisco, California, 97-98
Santa Monica, California, 88
science fiction, 53-54, 58-59, 65, 67, 70, 93-94
"The Science Screen" (column), 8, 33
Secret of the Submarine (film serial), 30
Serling, Rod, 9, 13, 15, 33-35
serials, motion picture, 30
The Seven Faces of Doctor Lao (film), 11, 16, 36-37
sexuality, 75-78, 82-84, 106
The Shadow (radio), 30
Shatner, William, 13, 15, 26, 36
Shaw, Irwin, 25
Simon, Adam, 12, 37
Skelton, Red, 32
Smokey Stover (cartoon), 30
Sohl, Jerry, 13, 34
Sorokin, Pitirim, 41
Speed Week, 9
The Spider (magazine), 31
spinal meningitis, 5, 14
sports cars—SEE: automobile racing
St. John, Al, 32
Star Trek (TV show), 36
Steinbeck, John, 25, 45
Stella Dallas (radio), 30
Summerville, Slim, 30, 32
Suspense (radio), 30
Svevo, Italo, 46
Swain, Mack, 32
Sydenham, Thomas, 106
Tarzan, 74

TITLES

*Works by Charles Beaumont
(unless otherwise noted)*

CHARACTERS

Ludlow, Henry, 90
Ludlow, Myrtle, 90
Lynch, Jackson, 92-93
Mainwaring, 89-90
Mallet, Mike, 55-56
Manassan, George, 112-113
Maple, Lydia, 77-78
March, Arnold, 103
Markeson, Gerald, 109
Markeson, Sylvan, 109
McDaniel, Ella, 42-45
McDaniel, Tom, 15, 44
McHugh, Rose-Ann, 57-58
Merriwell, Frank, 31
Meyers, 53-54
Mina, 69
Minchell, Henry, 68
Minchell, Jimmy, 68
Minchell, Madge, 68
Morrow, Mr., 97-98
Moseby, Lady Anastasia, 61
Musso, Gianinni, 78-79
Neely, 92
Nielson, Lars, 113-115
Niesen, Reverend Lorenzo, 44-45
Oakes, Robert, 64
Obadiah, 104-105
O'Hanlon, Professor, 58-59
O'Shaugnessy, Oliver, 80-81
Osterman, Hank, 72
Osterman, Ruth, 72
Paco, 71
Paige, Sheridan, 49-50
Parker, John S., 113
Paton, Harley, 15, 36, 4245
Pawnee Bill, 31
Peldo, Edna, 54-55
Peldo, Jake, 54-55
Peldo, Luther, 54-55
Peskin, Edmund, 85-86
Phillips, Agnes, 81-82
Phillips, Carlie Lee, 81-82
Phillips, Randolph, 81-82
Pierce, Eddie, 86

Pierce, Emma, 86
Pollet, Mr., 79-80
Prentice, Ann, 94-95
Prentice, Davey, 94-95
Prentice, Hank, 94-95
Protheroe, Captain, 102
Randall, Jessica, 88
Ransome, Allan, 35, 102-103
Ransome, Eileen, 102-103
Raphael, Ronald, 63
Richards, Alan, 34
Robert/Roberta, 96-97
Ryder, Waiter, Jr., 34-35, 84-85
Salvadori, 83-84
Santucci, Joseph William, 66
Savage, Doc, 31
Schmidt, Lorraine, 87
The Shadow, 31
Shipman, Verne, 4145
Silk, Dr., 104-105
Simms, Edward, 75-76
Simpson, Sid, 48-50
Smith, Mr., 35, 108
Solomon, 110
Son, 65
Sprool, Diggory, 107
Sprool, Emma (Hurlburt), 107
St. Claire, Mrs., 79
Takeena, 89-90
Talbot, Alan, 34-35, 84-85
Thomas, Miss, 95-96
Traskers, Elissa, 51-52
Valentine, Rocky, 34
Velasquez, Julio, 71
Volshak, 75
Washington, Cleota, 112-113
Washington, Willie, 112-113
Weber, 53-54
West, Abner, 15, 44-45
Wickwire, Jeremy, 34, 53-54
William (Pan), 78
Withers girl, 81
Woola, Princess of Sarboom, 74
Younger, Lonnie, 110

134

REFLECTIONS

In the depths of every heart there is a tomb and a dungeon, though the lights, the music, and revelry above may cause us to forget their existence, and the buried ones, or prisoners whom they hide. But sometimes, and oftenest at midnight, these dark receptacles are flung wide open.

—Nathaniel Hawthorne (1804-1864)

And Darkness and Decay and the Red Death held illimitable dominion over all.

—Edgar Allan Poe (1809-1849)

Life is our dictionary.

—Ralph Waldo Emerson (1803-1882)

With thinking we may be beside ourselves in a sane sense. By a conscious effort of the mind we can stand aloof from actions and their consequences; and all things, good and bad, go by us like a torrent.

—Henry David Thoreau (1817-1862)

135

ABOUT LEE PROSSER

LEE PROSSER has been writing for publication since 1963 and has over one thousand publications to his credit; additionally, he has been an educator, book store manager, medical records librarian, composer, among other pursuits. Born in Missouri on December 31, 1944, he has earned degrees in english, sociology, and social science. Some of his musical compositions are "Ramakrishna Waltz," "Baroque Fantasy for Piano, Cello, and Orchestra," "Lonesome Peter Blues," "Jesus Christ Canticle," "Jazz Lady Waltz." Among his numerous publications are *Dandelion Seeds: Eighteen Stories* (1974), *The Capricorn and Other Fantasy Stories* (1974), *Goodbye Lon Chaney, Jr., Goodbye* (novelette, 1977), *Desert Woman Visions: One Hundred Poems* (1987), *Jack Bimbo's Touring Circus Poems* (1988). He has contributed essays to *Reader's Guide to 20th Century Science Fiction* edited by Marilyn Fletcher, *Phoenix from the Ashes: The Literature of the Remade World* edited by Carl Yoke, and *New Encyclopedia of Science Fiction* edited by James Gunn. Prosser has written under the pseudonyms of Justin Willard Pinoak, A. A. Toms, Turyatita, and H. L. Shalloto. He has held a lifelong interest in Vedanta, Wicca, Shamanism, and Ancient Christianity. He was influenced early in his life in the teachings of Vedanta by Christopher Isherwood and W. D. Firestone, both of whom he knew personally. A trained sociologist, Prosser analyzes from a sociological perspective. Among his many interests are mountain and cave explorations, photography, travel, music, and shamanic drumming and healing techniques. Prosser lives with his wife in New Mexico. He is at present working on a book about Shamanism, Wicca, Ancient Christianity, and Vedanta.

136

www.ingramcontent.com/pod-product-compliance
Lightning Source LLC
LaVergne TN
LVHW091307080426
835510LV00007B/398